Ebenezer Kinnersley

Franklin's Friend

By J. A. Leo Lemay

Philadelphia
UNIVERSITY OF PENNSYLVANIA PRESS

7425
Printed in the United States of America

Preface

Ebenezer Kinnersley (1711–1778) first won fame when, in the middle of the hot Philadelphia summer of 1740, at the height of the Great Awakening, he attacked, from the pulpit of the Baptist Church, the emotional excesses of the popular revivalistic ministers. During the course of the Great Awakening, Kinnersley published five tracts, gradually moving from his condemnation of the manner of the revivalistic ministers and their audiences to his editorial in Franklin's *Pennsylvania Gazette* in January, 1748, where he pled for complete freedom of religion based on private judgment.

Ebenezer Kinnersley is best known as Franklin's collaborator in the experiments in electricity. Franklin wrote in his *Autobiography* that he suggested Kinnersley give lectures and that he drew up the first syllabus of Kinnersley's lectures. Kinnersley was not the first who gave popular lectures on electricity, nor was he the only one during the twenty-five years that he was most active—but no other lecturer was as popular, successful, or original as he. He was the greatest of the popular lecturers in colonial America (the ancestors of the nineteenth century lyceum movement). He was the greatest scientific popularizer of colonial America and the only person beside Franklin in the colonies who made significant contributions to the science of electricity.

This "master of words" who had "an Elegancy peculiar to himself" was the first Professor of English and Oratory at

5

the University of Pennsylvania (then the Philadelphia College). As such, he may have been the first person to teach English on the college level and probably was the first person to have the title Professor of English. In his career of over twenty years at the Philadelphia College, Academy, and Charitable School, he taught many of the leaders of Revolutionary America, and, following Franklin's plan, helped to introduce modern subjects into the classroom.

My two greatest debts are to my friends Alfred Owen Aldridge and Whitfield J. Bell, Jr. This study was undertaken at Dr. Aldridge's suggestion and, in an earlier form, presented as a Master's thesis at the University of Maryland. Dr. Whitfield J. Bell, Jr., has read the entire manuscript and I have profited by his suggestions—though the result would be far better had I followed them as closely as I should have. It is also a pleasure to thank Drs. Theodore Hornberger and I. Bernard Cohen for their kindness and encouragement.

The editor of *Isis,* Harry Woolf, has kindly given me permission to use part of my article, "Franklin and Kinnersley," in this study.

Contents

Illustrations

Kinnersley's advertisement   frontispiece

This advertisement, containing Kinnersley's syllabus of experiments (the usual form of his advertisement) on the front page of the *New York Gazette* for June 1, 1752, is an eloquent testimony to the effectiveness of his appeal as the greatest scientific popularizer of colonial America. The most advanced scientific information concerning electricity was set forth in topics such as "That it is intimately mixed with the Substance of all the other Fluids and Solids of our Globe" and "A Description and Explanation of Mr. *Muschenbrok's* wonderful Bottle." And one can easily imagine how entertaining the following "experiments" could be: "The Salute [kiss] repulsed by the Ladies Fire; or Fire darting from a Lady's Lips, so that she may defy any Person to salute her" or "A Piece of Money drawn out of a Person's Mouth in spite of his Teeth; yet without touching it, or offering him the least Violence."

In addition, the two recommendatory letters, telling of the writers' former prejudice against the scientists' presumptuous meddling with God's element, electricity, reveal the widespread opposition Kinnersley encountered. The writers, still seeming surprised, confess that Kinnersley has convinced them of the truth of the explanation of the electrical nature of lightning.

The reproduction has been made from the copy in the Library of Congress.

9

The Academy and New Building   facing p. 88

The original ink drawing from which this reproduction has been made is in the Du Simitiere Papers in the Library Company of Philadelphia.

The electric air thermometer, with a
melted lightning rod   Facing p. 100

Modern versions of this, known as the Kinnersley thermometer, are still used in electrical studies. The original drawing made by Kinnersley and sent to Franklin has been lost, but two contemporary engravings survive, one by J. Mynde, for the first appearance of Kinnersley's article, in the *Philosophical Transactions of the Royal Society* for the year 1763, and the other by I. Hulett, for the fourth English edition of Franklin's *Experiments and Observations on Electricity* (1769). I have chosen to reproduce the earlier engraving, by J. Mynde, partially because the other has been twice reproduced, recently in I. Bernard Cohen's *Benjamin Franklin's Experiments*.

Kinnersley also included a sketch of a lightning rod which had been struck by lightning and melted.

EBENEZER KINNERSLEY

Franklin's Friend

The Religious Career of
Ebenezer Kinnersley

1. FAMILY, AND LIFE TO 1740

EBENEZER KINNERSLEY was born November 30, 1711, in the
city of Gloucester, England.[1] His father, William Kinnersley,
the son of Richard and Mary Kinnersley, was born in 1669
at the Lynch, near Leominster in Eidsfield Parish,
Herefordshire, England. Ebenezer's mother was Sarah
(Turner) Kinnersley of Rofs in the same county. Before
Ebenezer was three years old, the family moved to America.[2]
They settled in Lower Dublin, Pennsylvania, where William
Kinnersley became an exhorter in the Pennepack (Lower
Dublin) Baptist Church. "It was in this quiet retired country,
on the banks of the beautiful Pennypek Creek, that young
Kinnersley's early life was passed—there he pursued his
studies under the supervision of a pious father, whose coun-
sels no doubt were instrumental in directing the attention of

---

[1] Morgan Edwards, *Materials Towards a History of the American
Baptists,* (Philadelphia, 1770), I, 15–16. Morgan Edwards was a
friend of Kinnersley. This is the best source for the early history of
the Baptists in Pennsylvania. The genealogical account given by
Edwards has been supplemented from the Kinnersley records in the
"Humphrey Family Bible": photostats in the Historical Society of
Pennsylvania.

[2] Sarah Kinnersley was admitted a member of the Pennepack
Church "upon a letter" on September 12, 1714. "Records of the
Pennepack Church," p. 413, Historical Society of Pennsylvania.

the young man to the higher concerns of religion."[3] Ebenezer Kinnersley was home-educated and, no doubt, to a large extent, self-educated.

The Reverend Abel Morgan had been minister of the Pennepack Baptist Church since 1711. He had William Kinnersley as his assistant; when Abel Morgan died on December 16, 1722, William Kinnersley, "who was a gifted brother, and very useful, regular man,"[4] continued to look after the church alone until June 17, 1726.[5] Then, Kinnersley "Being both aged and having several bodily infirmities,"[6] the Reverend Jenkin Jones was called from the church at Welsh Tract, in Newcastle, to be the minister. The Penne-pack Church had a thriving branch in Philadelphia, and it was to this branch tht Mr. Jones chose to devote most of his time.[7]

William Kinnersley continued to be as active as his health permitted. He remained Jenkin Jones's assistant minister, and his name is recorded at the Philadelphia Baptist Association meetings (which were held yearly after its foundation in 1707) in 1729 and 1731.[8] He probably went to these meetings every year when not prevented by his ailing health: the names of those attending were not recorded every year; and even in the years they were recorded, the list of names has

[3] Horatio Gates Jones, "Ebenezer Kinnersley," in William Buell Sprague's *Annals of the American Pulpit* (New York, 1860), VI, 45.
[4] Abram Dunn Gillette, *Minutes of the Philadelphia Baptist Association from A.D. 1707, to A.D. 1807* (Philadelphia, 1851), p. 12.
[5] Edwards, p. 15, gives the date as 1725 ; Gillette, p. 12, gives 1726 ; I have chosen the more definite date given by Horatio Gates Jones, *Historical Sketch of the Lower Dublin Baptist Church, Philadelphia, Pa., with notices of the pastors, &c.* (Morrisania, New York, 1869), p. 22.
[6] Gillette, p. 12.
[7] Jones, *Historical Sketch*, p. 22.
[8] Gillette, pp. 30 and 32.

been found incomplete.[9] William Kinnersley had another child, Mary, who was born August 20, 1715, and "who married into the Duffield and Hubbs families, and . . . raised . . . eight . . . children."[10] On February 13, 1734, William Kinnersley, sixty-three years of age, died and was buried at Pennepack.[11]

Ebenezer Kinnersley was baptized by the Reverend Jenkin Jones on September 6, 1735.[12] In 1739 he married Sarah Duffield, the daughter of Joseph and Hannah Duffield and the niece of the second wife of Colonel Jacob Duché, the prominent Philadelphia merchant.[13] About this time he moved to Philadelphia. I have been able to find no evidence for the reasonable claim that he earned his living by teaching;[14] Edward Bradley's will, dated March 22, 1744, reveals that Kinnersley was then a "shop-keeper."[15] It seems quite possible that Kinnersley worked for Jacob Duché in some position similar to this after he moved to Philadelphia. A

---

[9] Ebenezer Kinnersley, *A Letter to the Reverend the Ministers of the Baptist Congregations, in Pennsylvania, and the New Jerseys; containing Some Remarks on their Answers to Certain Queries, Proposed to Them, at their Annual Association Philadelphia, September 24, 1746* . . . (Philadelphia, [1747]). Hereafter cited as *Letter to the Baptist Ministers.* Here, Kinnersley wrote that because he had been ill, he was unable, contrary to his usual custom, to be with the ministers at their annual meeting. But the only time Kinnersley is recorded as attending the annual meeting was in 1738 (Gillette, p. 38).

[10] Her date of birth and name "Mary Hubbs" is given in the Humphrey Family Bible. The quotation is from Edwards, p. 15n.

[11] "Records of the Pennepack Church," p. 420.

[12] *Ibid.*

[13] Will of Joseph Duffield: Will Book "H", p. 214, Philadelphia Wills; and Edward Duffield Neill, "Rev. Jacob Duché," *The Pennsylvania Magazine of History and Biography,* II (1878), 61.

[14] Horace C. Richards, "Some Early American Physicists," American Philosophical Society, *Proceedings,* LXXXVI (1942), 25; and *Dictionary of American Biography.*

[15] Henry F. Waters, "Genealogical Gleanings in England," *New England Historical and Genealogical Register,* XLVII (1893), 118.

number of records exist which indicate that he handled business affairs for Duché and that he was called upon for the miscellaneous clerical work available to a well-educated man of integrity.[16]

He also served as assistant minister to Jenkin Jones until sometime after 1746. When Jenkin Jones preached at Lower Dublin, it is likely that Ebenezer Kinnersley preached in Philadelphia. It is recorded that "In the Rev. J——s's absence," on Sunday, July 6, 1740, Ebenezer Kinnersley preached in the Baptist Church in Philadelphia."[17] Had this been the first time Kinnersley preached, some reference to this fact would probably have turned up in his controversy with the Baptist Church. It also seems reasonable to suppose that he preached a number of times before and after his ordination in 1743. He probably had a position of some distinction in the church as early as 1738 when he was one of the representatives of the Pennepack Church at the meeting of the Philadelphia Baptist Association.[18]

2.   BACKGROUND OF THE GREAT AWAKENING

The Great Awakening was the first and perhaps the most intense large-scale religious revival in America. Part of the European pietistic movement, it also answered needs peculiar to America. In a revival, the conversions that New England's Covenant theology demanded were visibly won, and the impoverished but violent emotional life of a simple frontier

---

[16] See under "Kinnersley" in the manuscript collections of the American Philosophical Society, the Library Company of Philadelphia, and the Historical Society of Pennsylvania.

[17] Ebenezer Kinnersley, "A Letter from Ebenezer Kinnersley to his Friend in the Country," *Postscript* to the *Pennsylvania Gazette*, July 15, 1740.

[18] Gillette, p. 38.

people could find ample outlet. An early shadow of the Great Awakening was raised in New Jersey's Raritan Valley in 1720, when the Reverend Theodore J. Frelinghuysen, a pietistic minister of the Dutch Reformed Church, settled there. Frelinghuysen's "impassioned manner of preaching, his advocacy of inner religion in contrast to the mere outward performance of religious duties, and his attempts to bring about conversions soon brought a cleavage among his parishioners."[19] By 1726, Frelinghuysen had won his battle over his main opponent, Henricus Boel, and established himself and his revivalistic preaching in New Jersey. The cleavage from 1720 to 1726 in the four Dutch Reformed churches to which Frelinghuysen ministered prefigured the schisms and bitter feuds of the churches throughout America from 1740 to 1744.

In 1726 William Tennent became the Presbyterian minister at Neshaminy, Pennsylvania, established his "Log College," and began training revivalist ministers; in 1727 Jonathan Edwards was appointed minister of the church in Northampton, Massachusetts; in 1728 William Law's symptomatic *Serious Call to a Devout and Holy Life* was published. Perhaps the earliest manifestation of the Great Awakening ocurred in Northampton, in December, 1734, when Jonathan Edwards excited the people to a state of religious fervor by a series of sermons on justification by faith alone. In New Jersey, Frelinghuysen found allies in the graduates of the Log College who settled near New Brunswick; and by the late 1730's, these two influences combined with Aaron Burr in Newark to awaken revivalism in New Jersey.

---

[19] William Warren Sweet, *Religion in Colonial America* (New York, 1942), p. 275.

The conservative Presbyterian divines, alarmed by the influence of William Tennent's Log College, enacted laws in the Synod requiring all candidates for ordination to present diplomas either from New England or European colleges. At this time, John Rowland, a recent Log College graduate, was licensed at the first meeting of the newly formed New Brunswick Presbytery, a group composed of five evangelical ministers (the four sons of William Tennent and Samuel Blair— all Log College graduates). Rowland went to Maidenhead and preached. On September 19, 1738, members of the Maidenhead church complained to the Philadelphia Presbytery, which advised that "Rowland was not to be esteemed and improved as an orderly candidate of the ministery."[20] Rowland continued to preach, the matter was referred to the Synod, and, after an examination, he was chosen only as an evangelist.

"The greatest evangelist of his time and perhaps of all time,"[21] the Reverend George Whitefield, came to America in 1739. He landed at Lewes, Delaware, in August, and began his first America evangelistic tour in the region where Frelinghuysen and the Log College graduates had their greatest strength. Whitefield cooperated with any minister who espoused enthusiastic tendencies: William Tennent and John Rowland were soon his friends and admirers.

3.   KINNERSLEY AND THE GREAT AWAKENING

In 1740 the Great Awakening was at full strength. Notices in all colonial newspapers followed the amazingly successful tour of George Whitefield with excitement. A typical report

---

[20] Richard Webster, *A History of the Presbyterian Church in America* (Philadelphia, 1857), p. 470.
[21] Sweet, pp. 276-77.

appeared in Franklin's *Pennsylvania Gazette,* June 12, 1740—less than a month before Kinnersley attacked the emotional excesses which still characterize some revivalist preachers:

> During the Session of the *Presbyterian* Synod, which began on the 28th of the last Month, and continued to the third of this Instant, there were no less than 14 Sermons preached on *Society-Hill* to large Audiences, by the Rev. Messrs. the *Tennents,* Mr. *Davenport,* Mr. *Rowland* and Mr. *Blair,* besides what were deliver'd at the *Presbyterian* and *Baptist* Meetings, and Expoundings and Exhortations in private Houses. The Alteration in the Face of Religion here is altogether surprising. Never did the People show so great a Willingness to attend Sermons, nor the Preachers greater Zeal and Diligence in performing the Duties of their Function. Religion is become the Subject of most Conversations. No Books are in Request but those of Piety and Devotion; and instead of idle Songs and Ballads, the People are everywhere entertaining themselves with Psalms, Hymns and Spiritual Songs. All which, under God, is owing to the successful Labours of the Reverend Mr. *Whitfield.*
>
> On Sunday last, the Reverend Mr. *Gilbert Tennent,* preached four Times, viz. at Seven in the Morning on Society Hill, at 10 in the *Presbyterian* Meeting House, and 3 Afternoon in the *Baptist* Meeting House, and at Seven in the Evening on Society Hill again; at which last Sermon 'tis thought there were near 8000 People.

Kinnersley must have been disgusted with the antics of Davenport, Rowland, and Blair—but the worst was yet to come. At John Rowland's second sermon in the Baptist Church in Philadelphia, "The audience was sadly overcome by his description of their wholly-ruined condition as sinners; and the distress rose to such a pitch that Gilbert Tennent went to the pulpit stairs and cried out, 'Oh, brother Rowland,

is there no balm in Gilead?' "²² With this, Rowland changed
his manner and joyfully proclaimed the way to salvation.

This was on a Thursday evening. Ebenezer Kinnersley was
in the audience. John Rowland's deliberate working on the
emotions of the congregation enraged him. Three days later,
Sunday, July 6, 1740, the Reverend Jenkin Jones being away,
Kinnersley delivered the sermon at Philadelphia's Baptist
Church. He attacked the method and effects of the preaching
of George Whitefield and his followers, dramatically describ-
ing the hallucinations attending the revival:

> I am not against Preaching of Terror, in order to convince
> prophane, impenitent Sinners of their awful and tremendous
> Danger, provided it be prudently managed; but such Preaching
> as we have lately been entertained with, I do now openly
> profess my Abhorrence of it: It was unbecoming a Minister
> of the Gospel, and a Reproach to that Sacred Character: I
> mean those horrid Harangues you were entertained with from
> this Desk* (*By the Rev. Mr. Roland) last Thursday night,
> and once before. What Spirit Such Enthusiastick Ravings
> proceed from, I shall not attempt to determine; but this I am
> very sure of, that they proceed not from the Spirit of God, for
> our God is a God of Order, and not of such Confusion: Such
> whining, roaring Harangues, big with affected Nonsense, have
> no other Tendency, but to operate upon the foster Passions,
> and work them up to a warm Pitch of Enthusiasm, which
> when the Preacher has done, he has fully gain'd his End, and
> goes away rejoicing in his triumphant Conquests over weak
> Minds. . . . The Effects of such Preaching are very notorious
> in this Town; and Religion is sufficiently disgraced by it. Some
> are terrified to Distraction; others drove into Dispair; others
> wishing themselves in the same condition, but can't attain to
> it; while others are fill'd brim-full of Enthusiastic Raptures
> and Extasies, pretending to have large Communications from
> God; to have seen ravishing Visions; to have been encompass'd

---

²² Webster, p. 471.

as it were, with Flames of Lightning, and there to have beheld our Blessed Saviour nail'd to the Cross, and bleeding before their Eyes in particular for them![23]

The results, Kinnersley maintained, as well as the methods, were "at least" unchristian. In speaking of God "as a God of Order," Kinnersley revealed the eighteenth century Enlightenment viewpoint of his personal religion. Although this position is clearly present when he speaks of "rational religion" with its "native Charms and Comeliness," his emphasis in the tracts of 1740 is on the emotional excesses of the revivalists:

These and such like Enthusiastick Extravagancies some of our bigotted young Zealots (who are not as yet distracted) have run into; and a censorious uncharitable Spirit is becoming universal among them, pronouncing all to be in a State of Damnation, who have not seen and felt what they have. If these are the Fruits of the Spirit of God, or the Effects of Regeneration, then Christianity appears infinitely worse, and more detestable than ever its worst Enemies have been able to represent it: but I hope God will shortly make a visible Discovery of these Mysteries of Iniquity, and cause rational Religion to appear in its native Charms and Comeliness. And I think it is a Duty incumbent on every Christian Minister, publickly to oppose such distractive Preaching, and the dangerous Delusions that are propagated by it: For my Part, I make Conscience of it, tho' I expect to be uncharitably treated for my Pains, even to be branded with the odious Character of a *carnal unconverted* Pharisee; . . .

And he was. Kinnersley's sermon caused a violent, immediate reaction; "some of them shewed their Resentments by Running out of the Place of Worship in a most disorderly and tumultuous Manner."

On his return, the Reverend Jenkin Jones learned of the

---

[23] Kinnersley, "Letter." See above, note 17.

violent schism in his church. Monday, the day after his sermon, Kinnersley read over his notes for Jones. At that time Jones agreed with Kinnersley that the latter had not opposed "the powerful Doctrine of JESUS CHRIST, and the Reformation begun in this Place," but only "Mr. Rowland's artful and pernicious Way of Working upon the Passions." Jones said that he too disapproved of Rowland's manner.

However, in his sermon on Wednesday evening, the ninth of July, Jones, perhaps yielding to popular pressure, blamed Kinnersley for attacking the doctrine as well as the emotionalism of the revivalists.

On Saturday the twelfth, Kinnersley was tried at a church meeting for "endeavouring to vindicate the Honor and Credit of Religion"[24] and for "opposing the disorderly and unbecoming Manner of Mr. *Rowland's* Preaching." He was found guilty. Kinnersley claimed that "Judge and Jury were my fierce accusers, and unreasonably prejudiced both against my aforesaid Conduct, and whatever I could offer in my Defence: we were all Speakers and scarce any Hearers."

At his trial, Ebenezer Kinnersley charged the Reverend Jenkin Jones with telling "untruths": Jones had that past Monday agreed with Kinnersley's condemnation of the manner of the revivalists, and on Wednesday, speaking to the congregation, had told a different story. Kinnersley also claimed that Jones had shown "as great a Dislike in private Families, to what is blameable in Mr. Rowland's Preaching," as Kinnersley had done in public. And finally, Kinnersley reported that Jones had promised friends "that he would not speak any thing in publick against what" Kinnersley

---

[24] Irony, as in this passage, was one of Kinnersley's chief weapons in attacking his opponents.

"had done, tho' he was vehemently urg'd to it by many of his People."

At the conclusion of his trial, Kinnersley was asked that he make a "frank Confession" that he had done wrong and was heartily sorry for it. He replied that to do so would be to act contrary to both reason and conscience. What had he done that was wrong, he asked. The jury replied that he had no business to do what he had done and that by the effect he could see how harmful it was. Unconvinced by this reasoning, Kinnersley said the jury was unreasonable. He asked that Jenkin Jones "instance wherein I had opposed the powerful Doctrine of *Jesus Christ,* &c." In conclusion, he told the congregation that if they thought he had treated Jones in any way amiss, to prove their charges, "which they did not do, nor I believe ever will."

Kinnersley would not confess that he had done wrong, and the church judged him unworthy to communicate with the congregation on the following day, Sunday the thirteenth. Bitterly, Kinnersley adds "and I suppose, [I] shall never be admitted any more without some such hypocritical Confession, tho' there was not one Thing offered in order to convince me of my supposed Error, that carried the least Conviction in it or deserved any Regard."

Tuesday, July 15, Kinnersley, still angry over his treatment by the church, finished his "Letter from Ebenezer Kinnersley to a Friend in the Country." It was an angry summary of the story, rashly attacking the Reverend Jenkin Jones and slandering a number of the Baptist congregation: "The Foremost of the Gang [who rushed out of the church during Kinnersley's sermon], I am inform'd, was a Woman, who supports such a Character as Modesty forbids to mention; and one Fool has often times made many, so this infamous Leader was followed by a Multitude of

Negroes, and other Servants, among whom were some few of higher Stations, but not overburdened with Discretion." In typical eighteenth century polemic style, Kinnersley charged, *"Mr. J——s and Mr. R——d are* Welch *Men, and were it not for that National Distinction which is very observable in Mr.* Jones's *Conduct, he would scarce have been prevailed upon to use me* in the Manner he has done." And Kinnersley closed with a defence of the personal and angry tone of his "Letter":

> P.S. I should not have sent you this Letter in the Manner it now appears, were it not that my Character has been publickly and vilely aspersed by Mr. *J——s,* who has represented me as an Enemy to Reformation, a Disturber of the Church's Peace, an Instrument of the Devil, and an Opposer of the powerful Doctrine of *Jesus Christ,* and the most powerful Preachers of it; I have therefore exposed it to public View, that the World may judge whether I have merited such barbarous and unchristian Treatment at his Hands.

Kinnersley probably hoped that Franklin would print the "Letter" in the *Pennsylvania Gazette* for that Thursday, July 17. But Franklin, who prided himself on excluding "all Libelling and Personal Abuse" from his newspaper,[25] probably tried to dissuade him from publishing it. Kinnersley consequently complained that the printers of Philadelphia were suppressing the truth and favoring enthusiastic preaching.[26] Kinnersley's "Letter" was published on or shortly after July 24, as a *Postscript* to the *Pennsylvania Gazette* of that date. Franklin justified printing it in a "Statement of

---

[25] Max Farrand, ed., *Benjamin Franklin's Memoirs, Parallel Text Edition* (Berkeley and Los Angeles, 1949), p. 244.

[26] This surmise is, I believe, justified by the content of Franklin's preface. The preface is entitled "Statement of Editorial Policy" in Leonard W. Labaree, ed., and Whitfield J. Bell, Jr., assoc. ed., *The Papers of Benjamin Franklin* (New Haven, 1960), II, 259-61.

Editorial Policy," containing an argument for freedom of the press. In concluding his preface, Franklin wrote the following disclaimer:

'Tis true, where Invectives are contain'd in any Piece, there is no good-natur'd Printer but had much rather be employ'd in Work of another kind. However, tho' many personal Reflections be interwoven in the following Performance, yet as the Author *(who has subscrib'd his Name)* thought them necessary, to vindicate his own Conduct and Character, it is therefore hoped, on that Consideration, the Reader will excuse the Printer in publishing them.

To exonerate the printers of Philadelphia from the charge that they had "been guilty of great Partiality in favour of the Preaching lately admir'd among us," Franklin mentions that another press has just published "the Rev. Mr. Cumming's sermons against the Doctrines themselves." Archibald Cummings' work was entitled: *Faith Absolutely Necessary, But Not Sufficient to Salvation without Good Works.* This pamphlet consists of an introduction and two sermons published "in their own vindication" after they had been attacked by George Whitefield. As the title reveals, the tract illustrates the general movement in the colonies away from Calvinistic determinism toward an Arminian position. Cummings declares in his introduction, "Tho' our good Works are not required to make us capable of meriting Heaven, (that being impossible for frail, sinful Creatures) yet are they absolutely necessary to make us fit Objects, for the infinite Mercy of God in Christ to bestow Heaven on." And like Kinnersley, the Reverend Archibald Cummings especially objected to the emotionalism of the revivalists, saying that devotion raised by passion is "only momentary and vanishing." He argued that listening to the revivalists, the audience was "under the strongest Delusions imaginable, and mistake the wild Freaks of an over-heated Fancy, for the Suggestions of God's holy Spirit."[27]

With Cummings its rector, the Anglican Christ Church was the center of Philadelphia's opposition to the enthusiastic tendencies of the Great Awakening.[28] Kinnersley, denied communication with the Baptist Church for one day (Sunday, July 13), attended Christ Church during his controversy. His abandonment of the Baptist congregation became a minor *cause célèbre* in colonial Philadelphia, for Samuel Miller years after recorded a garbled version of the story: "Mr. Kinnersley was bred a Baptist, and was for some time a preacher of that denomination; but afterwards, taking some offence, he left the Baptist communion, laid aside his clerical character, and joined the Episcopal Church."[29] Another writer, commenting on Miller's report, says, "His wife was an Episcopalian, and probably his sometimes waiting on her to church, gave rise to the groundless report above mentioned."[30] Kinnersley's temporary attendance of Christ Church in the late summer and possibly early fall of 1740 is undoubtedly responsible for this false information. After the first heat of the controversy, Kinnersley inserted concili-

---

[27] Archibald Cummings, *Faith Absolutely Necessary, But Not Sufficient to Salvation without Good Works* (Philadelphia, 1740), pp. x-xi, xiv-xv.

[28] Cummings' obituary in the *Pennsylvania Gazette* for April 23, 1741, well illustrates Franklin's use of his newspaper for (what he considered) instruction. The anonymous obituary praises Cummings, saying that he was "universally esteem'd . . . especially for his Charity and Moderation towards all Religious Societies of differing Pursuasions." This attitude was not true of Cummings, who had just been embroiled in a controversy, but was part of Franklin's creed.

[29] Samuel Miller, *A Brief Retrospect of the Eighteenth Century* (New York, 1803), II, 354n.

[30] David Benedict, *A General History of the Baptist Denomination* (Boston, 1813), I, 588. This is one of the few published references to Sarah (Duffield) Kinnersley. No other writer has commented on her religion. It seems unlikely that she was actually an Episcopalian.

atory overtures in his tracts, and he was ordained in 1743—
therefore he probably was not long absent from communion
in the Baptist Church.[31]

On Monday, August 11, 1740, the congregation of Philadelphia's Baptist Church assembled in a meeting appointed
for the further consideration of Ebenezer Kinnersley's "great
and highly aggravated Crime, in publickly speaking my
Opinion, of the *Tragical Preaching* we had lately been entertained with, by that skillful ACTOR the most Powerful Mr.
R——d; and also in Publishing my aforesaid Letter."[32] The
congregation decided to follow the advice of one of the
elders: to choose a committee consisting of nine men who
would hear the evidence, weigh the matter, and give an
opinion for the church. Kinnersley caustically comments
that from "a Committee chosen who were *thought to be Men
of Probity,* it might reasonably have been expected, that
Truth would have stood some Chance to have fair play; and
that, according to the Principle among Printers,[33] it would
have prevailed over Falsehood; But notwithstanding all
rational Probability thereof, the Event has proved the
Contrary to be true."

The purpose of the committee was "to consider of and
endeavour to reconcile the uncomfortable Difference"
between Kinnersley and Jones. As it was "expedient that
some regular Order" be followed in the investigation,
Kinnersley devised a method that the committee agreed to
follow. He posed seven questions on doctrine, manner, and
conduct that related to his actions and the emotionalism of

---

[31] Edwards, p. 47, gives 1743 as the date of Kinnersley's ordination.
In view of Kinnersley's religious opinions and his controversies, it is
regrettable that nothing is known of his ordination.

[32] Ebenezer Kinnersley, *A Second Letter from Ebenezer Kinnersley
to His Friend in the Country* (Philadelphia, 1740).

[33] A reference to Franklin's "Statement of Editorial Policy."

the Great Awakening. The committee members agreed to judge him on the basis of their answers to his questions.

The first of Kinnersley's questions was "whether Mr. Rowland's manner of address to the Passions, will, upon the best Information you can have of it, appear Commendable or Blameable?" Kinnersley reports that as a result of their *"toilsome* Debates and most *discreet* Considerations," they returned the following *"nervous, Emphatical answer"—"we shall not here determine."* In his examination and criticism of their replies, Kinnersley notes that they "wisely Evaded" this question, "being Apprehensive, as I suppose, of the consequence of such a Determination; and therefore what they could not commend, they would not blame, lest it should too much contenance what I had done."

Kinnersley asked whether he "had not a Right, considered in the Place of a Preacher, publickly to speak my Opinion of a Practice so pernicious and universally surprising?" They replied, *"you being only a* gifted brother *upon Tryal, We presume you had not a sufficient Right to enter into such Controversies, without the Approbation of* the Elders of the Church." Criticising this reply, Kinnersley gives his first clear suggestion of a belief in the individual's private judgment:

> In their answer to the *Second,* there is a plain Begging of the Question, taking that for granted which cannot be allowed them; for what I did was only speaking My opinion of plain Matters of Fact, and not entering into a Controversy, as is falsely insinuated: But if I had, I can see no Reason why a *Gifted Brother* Might not be allow'd so to do, . . . Nor can I see any Reason why a Preacher, though he be but a Probationer, or as they were pleased to Phrase it, a *Gifted Brother* upon Tryal, should not be allowed to speak his own Opinion of Publick Disorders, without first having a License from the *Elders* of the Church, for thoughts, which should be free, to

be thus fetter'd and confin'd, would in my Opinion, be as intolerable a hardship as our Englishmen once suffer'd by a Licenser of the PRESS.

The third question Kinnersley asked was whether he really gave cause, merely by expressing disapproval of Rowland's manner, for the great offence that was taken. The committee said that it was an *"Occasion of Offence, but how great we shall not now Determine."* Kinnersley notes that here "they seem something Modest."

Did the Reverend Jenkin Jones act "agreeable either to Scripture Rule or common Civility, in publickly exclaiming against what I had thus done; Representing it in a very criminal Light, to the prejudice of my Character; not only as a Preacher, but as a private Christian, and to the great Discouragement of my future Progress, in any Part of the Ministerial Function?" The committee reported, *"As to what Mr.* Jones *said against you in Publick, we* could not *determine, for the Evidences do not agree, But We hope your Character will be recovered by a humble holy Life, and pure Doctrine, if again called to the public Ministry."* This question, said Kinnersley, they "slily evaded," and pretended they could not come to a decision, because the "Evidences did not agree." He adds a convincing indictment of the committee:

[It is surprising that men professing Christianity] should be guilty of such Partiality, as to let their Affections Pilot their Judgments, contrary to *Conscience, Justice, or Equity;* and resolve all Adventures to favour the Party, whom they Most respected. For though I told them over and over, that *I could prove the Matter of My Charges against Mr. Jones, by substantial and Credible Evidences;* and had them ready to produce, when ever it was insisted upon; yet they never put me to the proof of any one of them; and yet with *great Assurance* have told the Publick, that they consciously examined into this affair; whereas they only examined some Negative Evidences, who said that they could not determine whether Mr. Jones had publickly treated me as I had represented. And though one of the Committee did affirm, that to his certain knowledge Mr. *Jones was Culpable;* yet, because their *Negative evidence* and his *Affirmative* did not agree, they could not determine whether Mr. Jones had acted as became him or not. Nor were they willing to have any further Proof against him, for fear it would turn out to his disadvantage.

Kinnersley's fifth question was whether he did not have a right, after he had been publicly attacked, to publish a defense of himself? The members of the committee replied that they utterly condemned his publishing an account of the affair. This reply, Kinnersley contended, was "contrary to all Sense and Reason."

He next asked, "How far am I Blameable in publishing Mr. *Jones's* inconsistent Conduct in this Affair, seeing he does not deny the Matters of Fact, which I have charg'd him with; but only disapproves of the Manner in which they are represented, being unwilling they should be counted *Untruths;* because he thinks he saw just Cause to *alter his Mind,* and to act contrary both to *Truth* and his former *professed Intentions?"* The committee said that they would not define how far Kinnersley was to blame, but that it was *"a breach of Church-Discipline, as well as Christian Charity."* He replied that this "is easier conjectured than proved."

Finally, Kinnersley queried whether Jones's motives, or the reasons he could give for his conduct were "sufficient to justify what he has done?" They replied that it was necessary for Jones to do something in order to clear himself, "but how far he acted therein, we are not wholly satisfied."

In its conclusion, the committee admonished Kinnersley *"in the Bowels of Christian Love, to be cautious and well advised, before you enter into any more like Controversies; for we can do no less than judge you worthy of Reproof; receive the same from us in Love, and pray to God to enlighten your Understanding, and make you willing and ready to submit to the Church, in whatever you have acted disorderly; so with our Prayers to God, who is able to bring Good out of Evil, we remain your Brethren. . . ."*

Seven members of the nine-man committee signed the judgment.

These seven[34] also placed an advertisement in the *Pennsylvania Gazette* of August 14, 1740, claiming that the reflections cast on Reverend Jenkin Jones were in no way just, and that he was not in the least guilty of speaking the "untruths" alleged against him. They further said that the Baptist Church had taken no actions against Kinnersley except "at that meeting of the 12th of July last . . . after his non-compliance with their order, to desire him to forbear communicating the day ensuing, they being (not without cause) dissatisfied he should."

But Jenkin Jones, the committee, *and* the Baptist Church were no match for Kinnersley: he ridiculed them in his *Second Letter from Ebenezer Kinnersley to His Friend in the Country,* dated August 20, 1740. Andrew and William Bradford published this about two weeks after the committee's advertisement appeared in the *Pennsylvania Gazette.* In this tract, Kinnersley summarized the events in the dispute since his first "Letter" and attacked the committee's advertisement. He called it "a Piece of vile Interpolation," containing a number of statements not in the original judg-

---

[34] George Eaton, Thomas Potts, Thomas Dungan, John Hart, Robert Parsons, William Marchall [sic], and William Branson.

ment. The statement that "Those Reflections cast on Mr. Jones are no way Just; nor is he in the least guilty of speaking the Untruths alleg'd against him" was not in the report that was signed by the committee; nor were there any other words that had the same meaning. Kinnersley also points out that two persons who were members of the committee refused to sign the report when it was drawn up, but they "did afterwards see cause to alter their Minds and Clandestinely Subscrib'd their Names; when they had no More right so to do, than those who had Never been concern'd in it." And although Kinnersley does not bring it up, it seems significant to me that not all nine of the committee members signed the advertisement rebuking him.

Although Kinnersley was attending Archibald Cummings' Christ Church at this time, he did not want to make his separation from the Baptist Church irrevocable. In concluding his *Second Letter,* he wrote:

I desire that everybody would put the most favorable Construction on Mr. *Jones's* imprudence in particular; for I believe that he was inadvertently led into it, by the urgent Sollicitations of *Litigious* Advisers, and I heartily wish that all our Contention might now be buried in Oblivion, that Peace and Tranquility might again subsist among us, and that our future Conduct might be as acceptable to God, and so recommend us to the favour of Men, as if what is past has never happen'd.

Franklin and Bradford may have been partially responsible for the mild and reconciliatory tone in Kinnersley's final sentences. Kinnersley wrote in a postscript to his *Second Letter:*

The Publishing of this Letter (which I suppose you expected sooner) was for sometime delay'd on purpose, that my rash Condemmers might first have an Opportunity to do something by Way of public Recantation, which might justly have been expected: and something of the kind was carried to the Press, in order to be published in the *Gazette* of *August* 21. Num. 610. But for what reason it lies there so long conceal'd (to use one of their own Expressions) I shall not now Determine.

Kinnersley probably took his *Second Letter* to Franklin on the day he completed it, August 20. But from the above it seems that he had a misunderstanding with Franklin over some (imagined?) "public recantation" by his "rash condemmers." At any rate, Kinnersley changed publishers, putting his tract in Bradford's hands. Bradford advertised it in the *American Weekly Mercury* for August 28 as "Next Wednesday will be published." The following advertisement appeared in the *American Weekly Mercury* for September 4:

> Just Published, A Second Letter from Ebenezer Kinnersley, to his Friend in the Country, Shewing the Partiality and unjust Treatment he has met with from a Certain Committee whose Names &c. are inserted in the Pennsylvania Gazette, Number 609. To be sold by the Printers hereof and Mr. Kinnersly [sic] near the Sign of the George in Second Street. Price Three Pence.

Kinnersley's hint that a recantation by the committee was carried to Franklin seems unlikely: had this been done, the quarrel would probably have then come to an end. But two more tracts were published.

The first of these was an attack on Kinnersley "writ by some hackney Writer in Philadelphia, at the Instance and by the Instruction of Mr. Jones." It was announced in the *Pennsylvania Gazette* for September 11:

> Shortly will be published, *Some Remarks on Mr.* Ebenezer Kinnersley's *Two Letters to his Friend in the Country; together with a full Vindication of the Rev. Mr.* Jones, *Pastor, and the Committee of the Church under his Care, from the Aspersions and unjust Accusations of the said Mr.* Kinnersley.

Charles Evans[35] gives this title as No. 4605 and adds "Philadelphia: Printed by B. Franklin, 1740." However, the *Pennsylvania Gazette* of September 25, 1740, advertises:

> On Saturday next will be published, A LETTER to Mr. Ebenezer Kinnersley from his friend in the Country, in Answer to his two Letters lately published.

Evans gives this title as No. 4542 and adds "Philadelphia: Printed by B. Franklin, 1740." The *Pennsylvania Gazette* for October 2, 9, and 16, 1740, repeats this latter advertisement under the heading *"Just Published."* From this chronology it is evident that there never appeared the separate publication that Evans numbered 4605: it was only a pre-publication advertisement for [Jenkin Jones?], *A Letter to Mr. Ebenezer Kinnersley. . . .* Of course there are no copies of the false title, No. 4605; unfortunately, neither are there any known extant copies of No. 4542.

Kinnersley had the last word in his quarrel with Jenkin Jones and the Baptist Church. The *American Weekly Mercury* carried on October 16, 23, and 30, the following:

> Just Published, a Letter to the Rev. Mr. Jenkin Jones from Ebenezer Kinnersley, occasioned by a late Anonymous Paper, published under the Fiction of a Letter to him from his Friend in the Country; but is supposed to be writ by some hackney Writer in Philadelphia, at the instance and by the Instruction of Mr. Jones.

It is regrettable that there are no extant copies of this tract.

After October, the controversy that Kinnersley had started on July 6 by preaching against the excessive emotionalism of the Great Awakening disappears from the Philadelphia presses. In all probability, Kinnersley's open breach with the Philadelphia Baptist Church was healed shortly after this—but before long, the increasingly Calvin-

---

[35] Charles Evans, *American Bibliography* (Chicago, 1903–1960).

istic position of the Philadelphia Baptist Association was to clash with Kinnersley's rationalistic Enlightenment principles.

4. KINNERSLEY'S LATER RELIGIOUS CAREER

On November 13, 1740, Esther,[36] and on October 29, 1743, William[37] were born to Ebenezer and Sarah Kinnersley.

[36] Humphrey Bible and "Records of the Pennepack Church," p. 345, in the Historical Society of Pennsylvania. Esther Kinnersley married Joseph Shewell, a Philadelphia merchant, on April 22, 1765 *(Pennsylvania Archives,* 2d ser., VIII, 770), and became the mother of three children: Sarah, born March 8, 1767; Benjamin, born July 7, 1770; and Elizabeth, born March 30, 1772. Elizabeth, who, it seems, was the only one to marry, married Edward Swift on October 12, 1791 (Humphrey Bible Records); Elizabeth inherited her father's share in the Library Company of Philadelphia. It was transferred to her name on July 3, 1830 (MS, Historical Society of Pennsylvania).

[37] Humphrey Bible. He graduated from the Philadelphia Academy in 1761. His early notebook of studies at the Academy is in the Archives of the University of Pennsylvania. He began studying medicine at the Philadelphia College in 1770 (Joseph Carson, "History of the Medical Department of the University of Pennsylvania" VI, 11, in the College of Physicians of Philadelphia) under Dr. Samuel Duffield. On October 5, 1773, in a letter to Joseph Yeates, he wrote "and have hitherto met with success in all my operations both in physic and surgery." (This and a number of his other letters to Yeates are in the Historical Society of Pennsylvania). He became a doctor and served in the Revolutionary War: "Doct'r William Kinnersley is appointed surgeon to those Corps in Genl. Hands Brigade, not already provided, and is to be obeyed accordingly."—Orderly Book, Headquarters, Wyoming, July 25, 1779, recorded in the *Pennsylvania Archives,* 6th ser., XIV, 55. After the war he returned to Northumberland County where he had earlier bought 300 acres of land *(Pennsylvania Archives,* 3d ser., XXV, 200; and Mrs. Henry Rogers, "Abstracts of Wills and Administrations of Northumberland County," Genealogical Society of Pennsylvania, *Publications,* XIII (1938-39), 51–52). Later he lived in Mahoning Township and Moreland Township, County of Philadelphia *(Pennsylvania Archives,* 3d ser., XIX, 428; and XVI, 612). He died April 6, 1785, and left all his property to his mother, "in particular three Lotts in Northumberland" with the understanding that his mother

Kinnersley was active in Baptist Church of Philadelphia during the mid-1740's, hoping, probably, for a congregation of his own. He attended the yearly meetings of the Philadelphia Baptist Association regularly: ill in September of 1746, he complained that he was unable, contrary to his usual custom, to attend the Association meeting.[38] On May 15, 1746, the name of the Reverend Ebenezer Kinnersley appears just after that of the Reverend Jenkin Jones at the formal incorporation of Philadelphia's Baptist Church.[39]

But Kinnersley evidently came to be regarded by his Baptist brethren as too strong-minded, too individual—indeed, too radical—to have a congregation of his own. He seems never to have been offered one. In church circles, he had, doubtlessly, a belligerent record. As I will show below, his breach with Jenkin Jones was not completely healed after the end of their public dispute in 1740; his Baptist brethren were suspicious of a man who could leave his own

would divide them among the three children "of my late Sister Esther Shewell."—Will Book "T", p. 141, Philadelphia Wills.

An interesting sketch of him is given by Alexander Graydon, *Memoirs of a Life, Chiefly passed in Pennsylvania* (Harrisburgh, 1811), pp. 84–85: "of all men I have ever seen, he had the happiest knack of being gross without being disgusting, and consequently, of entertaining a company sunk below the point of attic refinement. Modest by nature, and unobtrusive, probably from a conviction that he thereby gave zest to his talents, he always suffered himself to be called upon for his songs, which he then accompanied with his violin, to the exquisite delight of his hearers. He possessed humor without grimace or buffoonery; and in the character of a drunken man, which he put on in some of his songs and which may be endured as an imitation, he was pronounced by Hallans to be unequaled. But unfortunately, the character became at length too much a real one; and it is to be lamented, that one whose exterior indicated a most ingenious disposition would prematurely close his career by habitual intemperance."

[38] Ebenezer Kinnersley, *Letter to the Baptist Ministers*, p. 17. For full citation, see above, note 9.

[39] Morgan Edwards, p. 44; and "Minute Book," under this date, in Philadelphia's First Baptist Church.

church and attend another; and he did not seem at all reluctant to attack in print the decisions of the entire Philadelphia Baptist Association, or to openly declare his own religious convictions in the *Pennsylvania Gazette*. Both the Baptists' suspicion of Kinnersley and his independent religious attitude are well illustrated in his *Letter to the Baptist Ministers*.

This pamphlet was occasioned by the answers the Philadelphia Baptist Association gave to a set of questions proposed by Reverend Jenkin Jones. These were evidently questions Jones and Kinnersley had previously argued. Jones placed them before the Association at a meeting held September 24, 1746—a meeting that Kinnersley, being ill, was unable to attend.[40] Kinnersley disagreed with their conclusions; and on January 25, 1747, he completed his *Letter to the Baptist Ministers:*

> Reverend Brethren,
>
> Having seen your Answers to some Queries laid before you, at your last ASSOCIATION, and duly considered them; I conceive that your Sentiments, in Relation to the Subjects therein treated of, are repugnant to the Word of God, which we profess to be the *only* Rule of Faith and Practice: and therefore I humbly offer to your serious Consideration the following *Remarks;* hoping they may prove the Means of discovering, to our mutual Satisfaction, on *which* Side the Mistake lies. [p. 3]

Kinnersley probably found an attack on himself in the first question proposed by Jenkin Jones—May candidates for the ministry whose qualifications have been approved be admitted to preach before they are ordained? Kinnersley's controversy in 1740 had arisen from a sermon that he

---

[40] On August 25, 1746, Kinnersley witnessed William and Sarah Branson's bequests of three properties to the Baptist Church. William Williams Keen, *The Bi-centennial Celebration of the Founding of the First Baptist Church of the City of Philadelphia* (Philadelphia, 1899), p. 184. Therefore, he probably was not ill before September.

preached before his ordination. The Association had answered yes, a candidate could, but added that he should be eager to enter the church when called, and that if he were not eager to do so:

> It is a *plain Indication of a Heady, Self-Will'd Obstinate, and Ungovernable Temper, in any* GIFTED BROTHER, *to refuse to exercise his* GIFT, *as the Church shall be inclined to call* HIM: *And it is a Specimen sufficient to foreshow what may be expected from such A Person if ordained.* [p. 16]

Kinnersley demanded if "this *fine* SPEECH" would not have come "with a much better Grace from a POPISH INQUISITION, than from an *Association* of BAPTIST MINISTERS!" Is this the way to treat a man who is "making a modest Use of the *Right of Private Judgment;* which is the very *Basis* of the *Protestant Reformation"?* He passionately alternates sarcasm with pleas:

> Will not the *next* Step be, to recommend *Excommunication* for *every Man,* that, in any Instance, *dared believe* other ways than the Church believes?——I know, that when Men *search* the *Scriptures; and follow them,* and not the *Traditions of the Elders;* it has been usual to meet with *hard Treatment.* But, I think that *You,* my *Brethren,* should be the *furthest of any,* from *discouraging Examinations* of this *Kind,* who count it your *Honour* in *some points,* to keep *closer* to the *Scriptures,* than *some Christians* who *differ* from *you;* and have always thought it *unkind,* to have *Reproaches,* and *hard Names* given, when *Scripture* and *Argument* would have been more proper to *inform* you, if you were under any *Mistakes.* [p. 16]

Kinnersley's plea for "the *Right of Private Judgment"* as the "very *Basis* of the *Protestant Reformation"* is a key to his religious beliefs. This passage clearly identifies him as a rationalist who believes in the absolute authority of the Bible—in effect, a deist who believes in the Bible.[41] The

---

[41] Conrad Wright isolates and defines a very similar position,

Bible, of course, had to be interpreted, and about the interpretation, fallible human minds could disagree. As Kinnersley's lectures on electricity will show, his conception of the
relation of science and religion is also rationalistic and
typically (though hardly exclusively) deistic.

The Philadelphia Baptist Association imprudently added
to its reply to Jones's first question an attack on Kinnersley:

> *It is surely running an imprudent Risque, to ordain to Office in*
> *the* Church of GOD, *such men as are of a fluctuating Temper,*
> *who, upon Offences, will behave Strangely, and frequent other*
> *Assemblies; &c. Though they may have some* fine *Endow-*
> *ments; yet they can hardly be deemed* Faithful Men. [p. 16]

Kinnersley believed that this referred to his attending Christ
Church in the late summer and fall of 1740. But through
irony and superior reasoning, he brings triumph out of the
rebuke:

> *Some* will have it that *this is a hint for Mr.* Jones, who *has*
> *frequented Mr.* Whitefield's Assemblies, &c. *and even behaved*
> *so* strangely, *as to neglect his* own, *and attend the other, two*
> Sundays *successively; one of which was the day he should*
> *have administered the* Sacraments *to his* own People. *Others*
> think it was intended for ME; *who, for some time, frequented*
> *another* Religious Assembly, *while I was unjustly excluded*
> *from* Communion *in our* own.—But your *intimating* that the
> *Person* you *aim* at, is so *happy* as to be *blessed* with *"some*
> *fine* ENDOWMENTS;" makes me rather choose to leave the
> *compliment* with Mr. *Jones,* than be so *arrogant* as to think it
> was *intended* for *Me.* It was *He* that proposed the *QUERIES;*
> and it is *possible* you might not be well *pleased with him,* for
> giving you so much TROUBLE. But, was it not *unkind,* to
> treat him with *Reproaches,* for laying his DIFFICULTIES
> before you, and desiring your OPINION and ADVICE? Had
> this any *Tendency to clear up* the POINT you had in Hand?

"supernatural rationalism." *The Beginnings of Unitarianism in
America* (Boston, 1955) pp. 3-4.

—But if, after all, this *gilded* PILL *was intended for* Me; who
was then *sick in my bed* and could not be with you as usual;
all that I shall say to it, *is this;* That if calling to Mind the
WEAKNESS and MISCONDUCT of my BRETHREN would
be of any *Service* in my present ENQUIRY, or would promote
the interest of CHRIST'S *Kingdom, of Truth* and *Righteous-
ness;* it would be *easy* to make *Reprisals:* for the *fairest*
CHARACTERS are not without *Blemishes.* But I desire
rather to *imitate* the Example of the *meek* REDEEMER; who
has taught me, *when I am reviled to forbear reviling again.*
[p. 17]

Despite the fact that he had preached before his ordination, Kinnersley felt that a person should not be admitted
to preach the gospel until he had been ordained. Kinnersley
asks whether investiture is of so little importance that it may
be dispensed with? If one can preach without ordination,
why not administer sacraments, baptize, etc.? If ordination
is not necessary before one begins to preach, why should it
be afterwards? Kinnersley argues that preaching should be
regarded in as sacred a light as baptizing.

The second question Jenkin Jones brought up was, May
persons be ruling elders or deacons before they are ordained?
The Association replied yes. Kinnersley disagreed. He
argued that they would have no authority unless they were
ordained. Are they deacons or not? If not, what authority
have they? If they are, how did they get their authority?
If the Association says the church gave it to them, he would
ask who gave the church authority to do so: "CHRIST
allows *none* to be admitted to *sacred Offices* in HIS *Church,*
until they have *first been proved and found* qualified; nor,
has HE appointed any Way for their being admitted then,
but by Ordination" [p. 21]. Underlying Kinnersley's seemingly conservative position on these two questions and the
following one is his belief in the absolute truth of the Scrip-

tures. He believes that the Bible forbade it; therefore he is against it.

The third question raised was whether women may be allowed to vote in the church. Kinnersley said that the silence enjoined on women cannot be absolute: they may make a public profession of their faith in church, tell the church when offended, testify as to matters of fact when called upon, and speak in their own behalf when wronged. He agreed that these are necessary—but added that they are matters of subjection and not pertinent to the issue, the issue being what women may do as judges, who sit to consider and determine matters in debate. He said that the ministers agree that women must be excluded from all degrees of teaching, ruling, governing, and leading. But how can they be and yet be allowed to vote? The case is not helped even though the women are to be mute while they vote. And if they are to be allowed to vote, their "reasons undoubtedly ought to be called for and heard, and maturely considered without contempt." In this expression, Kinnersley reveals that, contrary to first impression, he is not a misogynist at all, but one concerned more with the rational interpretation of the Scriptures than suffrage for women.

The conclusion to Kinnersley's *Letter to the Baptist Ministers* contains several characteristics of the Enlightenment mind (uniformitarianism, rationalistic individualism, and intellectual equalitarianism),[42] again showing where Kinnersley's intellectual affinities lay:

> . . . as your *Answers* to the Queries were read to all your *Congregations*, I desire that this *Letter* may also be read in like Manner; that all such under your care as are capable to

---

[42] Arthur O. Lovejoy, "The Parallel of Deism and Classicism," *Essays in the History of Ideas* (New York, 1960), pp. 78–98 ; reprinted from *Modern Philology*, XXIX (1932), 281–99.

judge for themselves may have the Opportunity to consider what has been said on *both* Sides of the Question. . . . Let us reverence no *Error* ever the more for its *gray Hairs;* or being a *Stranger*; nor treat it as the Son of GOD was, when *"he came unto his own, and they received him not."* . . . And if, after our most diligent Enquiries after truth, and Endeavours to inform and convince each other, we should still be obliged to differ in our Sentiments; then let us bear with each others' supposed Mistakes; . . . [p. 24]

It should be noted that "antipathy to 'enthusiasm' [i.e., excessive emotionalism] and originality" is another "characteristic idea-complex" of Enlightenment thinking. Kinnersley's reaction to the Great Awakening was typical of the Enlightenment mind.

The Philadelphia Association saw no reason to change its position, and Kinnersley, probably smarting under the implied (if not actual) condemnation of his unorthodox position, once again had recourse to his friend Benjamin Franklin. Kinnersley's article *"The Right of Private Judgment"* ran on the front page of the *Pennsylvania Gazette* for January 19, 1747/8.[43] It is easy to understand why Franklin,

---

[43] Reprinted in the *Boston Evening Post,* February 8, and in the *Maryland Gazette,* February 17, 1747/8. The complete editorial is reprinted as Appendix I. I attribute this anonymous editorial to Kinnersley mainly because of the number of phrases and clauses in it that are identical to those used in his earlier writings. In addition, the thought, style, and chronology of his quarrel all point to his authorship.

Note: Since this has been set in type I have discovered that "The Right of Private Judgment" first appeared in Jeremy Gridley's *American Magazine* in October, 1744, pp. 578–580. It appears to be the first of two articles (the other: "Of Uniformity in Religion, and the Right of private Judgment defended," *ibid.,* March, 1745, pp. 102–106) on the same subject and probably by the same author. Therefore, I now do not think that Kinnersley wrote the article; he probably was influenced by it. The author was perhaps Gridley himself; for similar statements by Gridley see Lyon N. Richardson, *A History of Early American Magazines, 1741–1789* (New York, 1931), p. 39n.

a deist, printed his friend's polemic for freedom in religion.

Kinnersley's editorial is his answer to the increasingly Calvinistic position of the Philadelphia Baptist Association and a terse statement of his religious ideas. Natural law philosophy, which provided the idealogical support for the American Revolution, is as clearly at work here as it is in the Declaration of Independence. Kinnersley's arguments for his religious beliefs, like Elisha Williams',[44] prefigure the political arguments of the Revolution. Kinnersley began, "The grand Basis of the Reformation and Support of the Protestant Causes, is the *Right of private Judgment.*" Private judgment is a "sacred and original," "an unalienable Right" of human nature. Since man is, by his "original Constitution, a moral and accountable Being," it must follow that "the Rights of Conscience are sacred and equal in all." As "every one is accountable for himself, he shall be allowed to reason, judge and determine, for himself." To do otherwise is to pretend that a "substitute" will stand and be judged in his place "at the righteous Tribunal of God." "In Matters that *purely* relate to Conscience, and do not *directly* affect the Security and Welfare of Societies," a man's "Sentiments and Conduct should be free and uncontroul'd."

Kinnersley again attacked the revivalistic ministers of the Great Awakening, those "insinuating crafty . . . bold Impostor[s], who expose people "to endless Delusions, to the most *stupid impious* and *hurtful* Superstition" and frighten them "out of their senses." The religious radicalism that resulted from a belief in the exercise of reason as a fundamental natural law is perhaps given its clearest statement

---

[44] Elisha Williams, *The Essential Rights and Liberties of Protestants. A Seasonable Plea for the Liberty of Conscience, and the Right of Private Judgment, in Matters of Religion* . . . (Boston, 1744).

here: "no Constitutions and Rules of civil society can be just, that are inconsistent with this Right [i.e., of private judgment]; nay farther . . . no true divine Revelation can either wholly destroy, or restrain and limit, the Exercise of it."

God as well as society is subject to reason.

The publication of *"The* Right *of* Private Judgment" marked the end of Kinnersley's religious career. He never again published any religious tracts; and I believe that this editorial and the *Letter to the Baptist Ministers* (both of which attacked the official Baptist position— so far as there might be said to be an official position) ruined any chance he may have had, after his bitter quarrel with the Philadelphia Baptist Church and Jenkin Jones, of securing a parish.

However, he was a minister and a distinguished member of the Baptist Church; as such, he was active in church affairs, preached from time to time, and assisted on at least one committee of importance. On February 23, 1758, the church "Agreed that Rev. Eb. Kinnersley be invited to preach for us till we be supplied; and that Rev. Jenkin Jones, Henry Woodrow, George Weed, and Lewis Rees do acquaint Mr. Kinnersley herewith." Three months later, May 23, 1758, "Mr. Jones Proposed to invite Mr. Kinnersley once more, the proposal was rejected—Then he proposed to invite Rev. B. Griffiths and Rev. Peterson Van Horne to assist him the following month. Granted."[45]

On August 11, 1760, the "following persons, viz: Mr. Ebenezer Kinnersley, Mr. Steven Anthony, Mr. Samuel Morgan, & Mr. Samuel Burklow, was likewise chosen to be a committee to settle the church affairs, & examine the state

---

[45] "Minute Book, February 4, 1757–July 1, 1769," First Baptist Church of Philadelphia.

of the church, purchases, gifts, and donation, given to the said church and get them well secured where they are not, and to settle other affairs, that shall come before them."[46] The committee met on August 11, September 1 and 16, 1760; and on April 9, May 28, and July 6, 1761. At the church meeting on September 15, 1760, it was decided that "Isaac Jones, Esq., Stephen Anthony, Ebenezer Kinnersley and ———— Woodron to receive in trust a conveyance of a part of the lot on which the meeting house stands, from John Holmes; and to draw up a letter to invite Mr. Edwards[47] to come over, or any other gentleman of like character, to take up ministerial charge of the church." On December 8, 1760, the church records reveal that "Mr. S. Morgan promises to meet Eb. Kinnersley and Wm Ball at the house of the latter on Tuesday next to settle his account." The last record of Kinnersley's preaching is in the Minute Book: on May 5, 1764, the church voted that "Deacons Wescott and Moor are appointed to wait on Mr. Kinnersley and request him to preach for us the 3d Sunday in May next."

Two other accounts show that the Baptist Church recognized Kinnersley as one of their most distinguished members. On November 5, 1763, Morgan Edwards and Ebenezer Kinnersley were appointed "to draw up an address to the New Governor in the name and behalf of the church; and that Mr. Isaac Jones do accompany them in presenting said address." A similar document, sent to Richard Penn when he became Lieutenant-Governor, was published in the *Pennsylvania Gazette*, November 21, 1771:

---

[46] A quotation from the committee minutes, which are loose pages in the Minute Book cited above. A similar statement is in the Minute Book under the same date.

[47] On June 3, 1761, the Reverend "Morgan Edwards received as a member and minister of the church." Minute Book.

To the Honourable RICHARD PENN, Esq. . . .
May it please your HONOUR,
We, the Baptist Ministers in Philadelphia, for ourselves, and the Congregation to which we belong, beg Leave to address your Honour with our Gratulations on˙your being appointed our Governor, and on your safe Arrival to this City. We sincerely wish you all Happiness; and hope ever to demean ourselves, so as not to become unworthy a Continuance of that Benevolence and Protection which have hitherto been extended to us (in common with other religious Societies) by your honourable Family.

Signed by Order
Morgan Edwards
Ebenezer Kinnersley

Religious opposition to the Great Awakening stemmed from, basically, two groups: supporters of the *status quo* (e.g., Jonathan Boucher, the Presbyterian Synod that censured John Rowland, and Jonathan Edwards's church at Northanpton) or, in short, conservatives; and the rationalists (including deists), men who opposed the Great Awakening because it seemed to deny an approach to religion through the reason.[48] Most of the rationalists, like Charles Chauncey and Jonathan Mayhew, have become associated with Arminianism and the rise of Unitarianism, and their bold self-assurance has been recognized as a characteristic of the leaders of Revolutionary America. Kinnersley belongs in this group. His opposition to the Great Awakening (based on the right and the necessity for the individual himself to approach and interpret God, his belief in the "Charms and Comeliness" of rational religion, and his basic natural law

---

[48] Cf. Leonard Woods Labaree, "Pulpit and Broadcloth," in *Conservatism in Early American History* (Ithaca, New York, 1959). These two attitudes were often found in the same person: see Carl Bridenbaugh, ed., *Gentleman's Progress ; The Itinerarium of Dr. Alexander Hamilton, 1744* (Chapel Hill, 1948).

philosophy) antedates the more famous arguments of his contemporaries, Chauncey and Mayhew.[49]

[49] Cf. Edwin Scott Gaustad, *The Great Awakening in New England* (New York, 1957), pp. 86–88 ; and Perry Miller, *The American Puritans* (New York, 1956), pp. 137–42.

II   The Early Scientific Career of Ebenezer Kinnersley

1. THE INTRODUCTION OF ELECTRICITY INTO THE COLONIES

AN ACCOUNT of the introduction of electricity into the colonies will clear up the disputed question of the date and source of Franklin's introduction to electricity, show the achievements of the itinerant lecturers on electricity who sprang up in Boston in the summer of 1747 (and who were the ancestors of the nineteenth century lyceum movement— besides playing themselves no mean role in American culture), and set Kinnersley's role in proper perspective.

Although electricity was mentioned in the science course at Harvard in the seventeenth century,[1] and perhaps at William and Mary College after the establishment of the chair of Natural Philosophy and Mathematics in 1712,[2] it was probably not until 1726, when Isaac Greenwood gave his lectures and demonstrations in Boston, that the colonists were introduced to experiments in electricity. The third lecture of Greenwood's popular science course consisted of a number of "various Experiments concerning Electrical

[1] Samuel Eliot Morison, *Harvard College in the Seventeenth Century* (Cambridge, Massachusetts, 1936), I, 242–43.
[2] Galen W. Ewing, "Early Teaching of Science at the College of William and Mary in Virginia," *Journal of Chemical Education*, XV (1938), 4.

48

Attraction, and Repulsion."[3] Greenwood's experiments may not have been very effective, for there is no record that he excited any interest in electricity. Although Franklin doubtlessly saw Greenwood's lectures when the latter (who lectured in Boston, Philadelphia, and Charleston[4]) was in Philadelphia in 1740, Franklin does not mention Greenwood in writing of his introduction to electricity.

It was Dr. Archibald Spencer[5] who first excited real interest in electricity among the colonists. He introduced them to the marvels of electricity in Boston in the summer of 1743. Kinnersley probably saw his lectures in Philadelphia, where Dr. Spencer spent the spring and summer of 1744.[6] But Kinnersley's introduction to the study of electricity as an experimental science probably began with his participation in the experiments that Franklin devised and carried out in his home. Franklin wrote:

> I eagerly seized the Opportunity of repeating what I had seen at Boston, and by much Practice acquired great Readiness in performing those also which we had an Account of from England, adding a Number of new Ones. I say much Practice, for my House was continually full for some time, with People who came to see these new Wonders. To divide a little this Incumbrance among my Friends, I caused a Number of similar Tubes to be blown at our Glass-House, with

---

[3] Isaac Greenwood, *An Experimental Course of Mechanical Philosophy* (Boston, 1726), p. 2. Greenwood was the first Hollis Professor of mathematics at Harvard (1727–1738).

[4] His lecture advertisements are in the *Boston Gazette*, December 5 and 26, 1726; July 15 and 22, 1734; April 2 and 9, 1739; *Pennsylvania Gazette*, June 5, 1740; and *South Carolina Gazette*, December 31, 1744, and January 14, 1745.

[5] Previously misidentified as Dr. "Adam" Spencer. See J. A. Leo Lemay, "Franklin's 'Dr. Spence': the Reverend Archibald Spencer (c. 1698–1760), M.D.," *Maryland Historical Magazine*, LIX (1964).

[6] *Boston Evening Post*, May 30 and August 1, 1743; *Pennsylvania Gazette*, April 26, May 3, and July 26, 1744.

which they furnish'd themselves, so that we had at length several Performers. Among these the principal was Mr. Kinnersley, an ingenious Neighbour, who being out of Business, I encouraged to undertake showing the Experiments for Money. . . .[7]

Spencer "surpriz'd and pleas'd" the colonists with his experiments in electricity. But I believe that Franklin, contrary to what he implies here, was not started on his career in electricity by Dr. Spencer. Spencer aroused the interest of some colonists in electricity, and that was all. A distinction should be made between Franklin's being entertained by a surprising display of the marvels of electricity and his introduction to electricity as an experimental scientist. It was Peter Collinson who introduced the colonists to the experimental study of electricity, and this was done a year earlier and in a different way than has hitherto been suspected.[8]

Franklin commented on his introduction to electricity in several places. The earliest was in his letter to Peter Collinson, dated March 28, 1747. Franklin wrote: "Your kind present of an electric tube, with directions for using it, has put several of us on making electrical experiments. . . ."[9] But the most complete and important record of his introduction to electricity was in a letter to Michael Collinson, the son of Peter Collinson, who had recently died. Franklin's letter was meant for possible inclusion in a tribute to

---

[7] Max Farrand, ed., *Benjamin Franklin's Memoirs, Parallel Text Edition* (Berkeley and Los Angeles, 1949), p. 380.

[8] In "Franklin's Introduction to Electricity," *Isis*, XLVI (1955), 29–35, N. H. de V. Heathcote has argued that Collinson introduced Franklin to electricity.

[9] Leonard W. Labaree, ed., and Whitfield J. Bell, Jr., assoc. ed., *The Papers of Benjamin Franklin*, III (New Haven, 1960), 118 ; see also the letter to Collinson dated July 29, 1750, which begins with essentially the same words, *ibid.*, IV, 9.

Peter Collinson that his son was preparing for publication. Albert Henry Smyth noted, "Peter Collinson died August 11, 1768; Michael Collinson published 'Some Account of Peter Collinson,' in 1770. This letter was written late in 1768 or at the beginning of 1769."[10] Franklin began his last paragraph:

> During the same time [i.e., from 1730 to Collinson's death] he transmitted to the Directors [of the Library Company of Philadelphia] the earliest accounts of every new European Improvement in Agriculture and the Arts, and every philosophical Discovery; among which, in 1745, he sent over an account of the new German Experiments in Electricity, together with a Glass Tube, and some Directions for using it, so as to repeat those Experiments. This was the first Notice I had of that curious Subject, which I afterwards prosecuted with some Diligence, being encouraged by the friendly Reception he gave to the Letters I wrote to him upon it.[11]

For reasons that will be discussed below, I believe that this letter contains an accurate description of Franklin's introduction to the experimental study of electricity.

Somewhat over two years later, in England, Franklin made some notes for his projected *Memoirs*. He wrote:

> Go again to Boston in 1743. See Dr. Spence. Whitfield. My Connection with him. His Generosity to me. my returns. Church Differences. My part in them. Propose a College. not then prosecuted. Proposed and establish a Philosophical Society. War. Electricity. my first knowledge of it. Partnership with D Hall. . . .[12]

Here also, Franklin did not couple "Dr. Spence" (Dr. Archibald Spencer) with his first introduction to electricity. Why then is Spencer important enough for mention at all?

[10] Albert Henry Smyth, *The Writings of Benjamin Franklin* (New York, 1905-1907), V, 185.

[11] *Ibid.*, pp. 185–186.

[12] Farrand, p. 420.

Spencer astonished and interested Franklin with his electrical experiments. But because Franklin did not begin his own studies in electricity as a result of witnessing Spencer's lectures, he did not in his earlier recollections couple his introduction to electricity with Spencer. Spencer's role, I believe, was confined to arousing Franklin's interest in electricity.

The final two mentions of his introduction to electricity are in that part of his *Memoirs* written in America in 1788–1789, when he was eighty-two years old, at least seventeen years after he wrote the "Notes," nineteen years after he wrote to Michael Collinson, and well over forty years after his introduction to electricity. He wrote:

> When I disengag'd myself as above mentioned from private Business, I flatter'd myself that by the sufficient tho' moderate Fortune I had acquir'd, I had secur'd Leisure during the rest of my Life, for Philosophical Studies and Amusements; I purchas'd all Dr. Spence's Apparatus, who had come from England to lecture here ["in experimental Phil." is crossed out]; and I proceeded in my Electrical Experiments with great Alacrity . . .[13]

Although it is quite likely that Franklin purchased Dr. Archibald Spencer's apparatus,[14] he probably didn't do so until January, 1754, when he visited Annapolis.[15] Spencer gave his course of experimental philosophy as late as 1750 and had no apparatus when he died in 1760.[16] If Franklin

---

[13] *Ibid.*, pp. 300 and 302.

[14] I. Bernard Cohen, "Benjamin Franklin and the Mysterious 'Dr. Spence': the Date and Source of Franklin's Interest in Electricity," *Journal of the Franklin Institute*, CCXXXV (1943), 19–20, attempts, I believe with success, to identify some of the apparatus that Franklin bought from Spencer.

[15] *Maryland Gazette,* January 17, 1754.

[16] *Maryland Gazette,* September 26, 1750; Maryland Hall of Records, Probate Records, Inventories, 1763 Anne Arundel, Liber 81, folio 275.

used Spencer's apparatus in performing his early experiments, he must have purchased it when Spencer was in Philadelphia in 1744–1745. It seems extremely unlikely that Spencer would sell his apparatus while on a lecture tour— and he lectured in Williamsburg after he left Philadelphia.[17] It was probably only after Spencer was ordained and had a living (All Hallows, Anne Arundel County, Maryland) in the fall of 1751, that he sold his apparatus. Therefore, Spencer's apparatus was probably not instrumental in Franklin's early electrical research.

Franklin's final mention of his introduction to electricity has previously been generally credited:

> In 1746 being at Boston, I met there with a Dr. Spence, who was lately arrived from Scotland, and show'd me some electric Experiments. They were imperfectly perform'd, as he was not very expert; but being on a Subject quite new to me, they equally surpriz'd and pleas'd me. Soon after my Return to Philadelphia, our Library Company receiv'd from Mr. Peter Colinson, F.R.S. of London a Present of a Glass Tube, with some Account of the Use of it in making such Experiments. I eagerly seized the Opportunity of repeating what I had seen at Boston, and by much Practice acquir'd great Readiness in performing those also which we had an Account of from England. . . .[18]

As I. Bernard Cohen has shown,[19] it was in 1743 that Franklin met Dr. Spencer in Boston, but the date 1746 has been accepted as the date Franklin received the tube and instructions from Collinson.[20]

Not only was Franklin in good health and twenty years

[17] *Virginia Gazette,* January 9, 1745/6.
[18] Farrand, p. 380.
[19] Cohen, p. 4.
[20] E.g., Heathcote, p. 30; James Parton, *Life and Times of Benjamin Franklin* (Boston, 1864), I, 277; Carl Van Doren, *Benjamin Franklin* (New York, 1938), p. 155.

younger when he cited the date as 1745 in his letter to
Michael Collinson, but he there places the emphasis on that
part of Collinson's communication which I believe, deserves
it: "he sent over an account of the new German Experiments in Electricity, together with a Glass Tube, and some
Directions for using it, so as to repeat those Experiments."
It was the "account of the new German experiments" sent
him by Collinson that supplied Franklin with a solid foundation in the contemporary electrical knowledge (contrary to
the myth of the ignorant genius inventing in the savage
wilderness) and fired him and, independently, William
Claggett (who will be discussed below) with the zeal for
electrical experimentation that spread throughout the
colonies.

"An historical account of the wonderful discoveries, made
in Germany, &c concerning Electricity" appeared in the
Gentleman's Magazine for April, 1745.[21] I believe that Peter
Collinson, in 1745, sent Franklin an annotated copy of this
article, together with a glass tube and some directions for
using it. The article is a historical and bibliographical survey
of the recent advancements in electricity, with evaluative
comments, interpretations, and speculations. It is also a
popular account of the lecturers who had, in the last two
years, become the vogue in Europe:

And from the year 1743 they ["the German naturalists"] discover'd phenomena, so surprising as to awaken the indolent
curiosity of the public, the ladies and people of quality, who
never regard natural philosophy but when it works miracles.
Electricity became all the subject in vogue, princes were will-

---

[21] [William Watson?], "An historical account of the wonderful
discoveries, made in Germany, &c. concerning Electricity," *Gentleman's Magazine,* XV (April, 1745), 193–97. This important article
was overlooked by Paul Fleury Mottelay, *Bibliographical History
of Electricity and Magnetism* (London, 1922).

ing to see this new fire which a man produced from himself, which did not descend from heaven. Could one believe that a lady's finger, that her whalebone petticoat, should send forth flashes of true lightning, and that such charming lips could set on fire a house? The ladies were sensible of this new privilege of kindling fires without any poetical figure, or hyperbole, and resorted from all parts to the publick lectures of natural philosophy, which by that means became brilliant assemblies.[22]

The author of "An historical account" made some perceptive suggestions concerning the qualities lightning and electricity have in common:

Could it have been thought that the virtue, or current of the electric matter, so moveable and incapable of rest, could so tenaciously adhere to the silken cord, and not be dissipated and lost in air? Lightning has pretty much the same qualities, for it generally runs over the whole length of the solid bodies which it strikes, and it has been seen to descend along the wire of a steeple-clock from top to bottom, and the threads of the wire have been found at the bottom of the steeple, melted into thousands of small bits. This is not the only property which lightning has in common with electricity.[23]

Franklin, quoting his "minutes" he "used to keep of the experiments" he made, in his letter to Dr. John Lining dated March 18, 1755, shows that he arrived at his famous conclusion from a consideration of these same evidences in conjunction with more recent knowledge:

"Nov. 7, 1749. Electrical fluid agrees with lightning in these particulars: 1. Giving light. 2. Colour of the light. 3. Crooked direction. 4. Swift motion. 5. Being conducted by metals. 6. Crack or noise in exploding. 7. Subsisting in water or ice. 8. Rending bodies it passes through. 9. Destroying animals. 10. Melting metals. 11. Firing inflammable substances. 12.

---

[22] "An historical account," p. 194a&b.
[23] *Ibid.*, p. 193a&b.

Sulphureous smell. The electric fluid is attracted by points. We do not know whether this property is in lightning. But since they agree in all the particulars wherein we can already compare them, is it not probable they agree likewise in this? Let the experiment be made."[24]

If William Watson (probably, at that time, the best authority on electricity in England) wrote "An historical account," it would help to explain why in addition to receiving Franklin's work "in as laudatory a manner as possible," he also "advanced the view that Franklin's ideas were merely the same as his own."[25]

"An historical account" is the most enjoyable article concerning electricity I have read. Its hints of possibilities for research, and glowing descriptions of the possibilities of electricity excited such diverse minds as John Winthrop (Harvard's second Hollis professor) and William Claggett, the clock-maker, as well as Benjamin Franklin: "Electricity is a vast country, of which we know only some bordering provinces; it is yet unseasonable to give a map of it, and pretend to assign the laws by which it is governed."[26] The article concludes:

These new experiments being made public in your book, it is to be hoped that our philosophers will soon add some improvements by new ratiocinations, new circumstances, and perhaps by new discoveries. It has been already discover'd, or believ'd to be so, that electricity accelerates the motion of water in a pipe, and that it quickens the pulse. There are hopes of finding in it a remedy for the sciatica or palsy. Mess. *Lange* and *Kruger*, professors at *Hall*, and Mess. *Segner* and *Hoffman* at *Gottingen*, and several other learned men, have made experiments of this miraculous fire, and we are in

---

[24] Labaree, V, 524.
[25] I. Bernard Cohen, *Benjamin Franklin's Experiments* (Cambridge, Massachusetts, 1941), p. 95.
[26] "An historical account," p. 195a.

a fair way of soon becoming as well acquainted with that terrible element, as with air since the invention of the air-pump.

The study of nature amply recompenses men for their trouble. What astonishing discoveries have been made within these four years! The polypus on one hand, as incredible as a prodigy, and the electric fire on the other, as surprising as a miracle.[27]

In 1745, Peter Collinson, fascinated with electricity, sent annotated articles to his friends in the colonies. On March 30, 1745, he wrote to Franklin's friend Cadwalader Colden:

the Surprising Phenomena of the Polypus Entertain'd the Curious for a year or Two past but Now the Vertuosi of Europe are taken up in Electrical Experiments,[25] and what can be more Astonishing than that the Base rubing of a Glass Tube Should Investigate a Person with Electric Fire. He is not Touched by the Tube but the Subtile Effluvia that Flies from it pervades Every pore and renders him what Wee call Electrified for then Lett him touch Spirits of Wine & the Spark of fire that flies from his finger on the touch will Sett the Spirits in flame. . . .[29]

In view of Collinson's interest in electricity, it seems improbable that he would not have communicated the electrical experiments to his friends in Philadelphia. On August 3, 1747, Collinson sent an annotated article to Colden:

As the Surprising phenomenon of Electricity Engages the Vertuosi in All Europe I here Send you for the Present what has been done in France & with us, I have marked those Experiments that I have felt & can vouch for the Facts—but

---

[27] *Ibid.*, p. 197a&b.
[28] The similarity of this clause to the closing of "An historical account" suggests that Collinson had read the article.
[29] *The Letters and Papers of Cadwalader Colden* (New York Historical Society, *Collections* for 1917–1923, 1934, 1935), III (for 1919), 110.

there is a great Variety of others too Long to tell you in a Letter.[30]

Nor was Colden his only friend in America he sent articles to: in the last paragraph of this letter to Colden, Collinson wrote, "After our Worthy friend Mr. [James] Alexander has perused the Electrical papers I have desired to oblige you with the perusal of them."[31]

"An historical account," reprinted in the *American Magazine* for December, 1745,[32] immediately interested a number of men in Newport (one of the places where Dr. Archibald Spencer seems to have lectured).[33] The *Boston Evening Post* for March 3, 1746, carried this notice:

> Extract of a Letter from Newport, February 28, 1745/6.
>
> The wonderful account (in the Magazine) of the surprising Effects of Electricity, as lately discovered in several Parts of Europe, having raised the Curiosity of several Gentlemen here, Mr. William Claggett, Watch-maker, has fixed a Machine, by which a great Variety of those Experiments have been repeated, to the Astonishment of the Spectators.[34]

On May 10, 1746, John Winthrop at Harvard devoted his 26th lecture in a course of "Philosophical Lectures" to electricity. He defined "Electrics" and "non-Electrics" and showed an up-to-date knowledge of electricity. Such sentences as "This Electricity Since the Year 1743 has made a Considerable noise in the World upon which it's supposed several of the (at present hidden) Phaenomina of Nature Depend" suggest Winthrop's familiarity with "An historical

---

[30] *Ibid.,* p. 237.

[31] *Ibid.*

[32] *American Magazine and Historical Chronicle,* II (December, 1745), 530–37.

[33] Carl Bridenbaugh, ed., *Gentleman's Progress, The Itinerarium of Dr. Alexander Hamilton, 1744* (Chapel Hill, 1948), p. 189.

[34] This also appeared in the *American Magazine and Historical Chronicle,* III (January, 1746), 96.

account."[35] And on December 29, 1746, the Boston *Evening Post* carried a notice of Claggett's progress in electricity:

> We hear from Newport of Rhode Island, that Mr. William Claggett of that Town, has at last succeeded so far in the Electrical Experiments, as to set Fire to Spirits of Wine, the most satisfactory and difficult of all.

That "An historical account" inspired Claggett is a matter of record—in my opinion, it was also Franklin's inspiration.

To sum up Franklin's introduction to electricity: Collinson, interested in electricity by March of 1745, sent his correspondents annotated articles, and had been corresponding with Franklin for some time. Franklin wrote to Michael Collinson that Peter Collinson "in 1745 . . . sent over an account of the new German Experiments in Electricity, together with a Glass tube, and some Directions for using it, so as to repeat those Experiments." Not only is "An historical account" a fascinating and inspiring article, it is the only "account of the new German Experiments" that appears in the popular English magazines or *Philosophical Transactions* between 1743 and 1747. Collinson sent Franklin "An historical account" with his annotations and a glass tube in the spring of 1745, and thus started Franklin on his scientific career in electricity. Of course Franklin was indebted to the many articles in English and Continental publications on electricity that appeared after the summer of 1745—but by then he was already absorbed in his own experiments.[36]

---

[35] There is a manuscript "Summary of a course of Philosophical Lectures" by a student of Winthrop in the Massachusetts Historical Society. I have examined Professor Theodore Hornberger's microfilm of it. Cf. I. Bernard Cohen, *Some Early Tools of American Science* (Cambridge, Massachusetts, 1950), p. 43.

[36] Cf. Lloyd Espenschied, "The Electrical Flare of the 1740's," *Electrical Engineering*, LXXIV (1955), 392–97; and "More on Franklin's Introduction to Electricity," *Isis*, XLVI (1955), 280–81.

2. THE EARLY LECTURERS

After William Claggett gained sufficient skill in electrical experiments, he found that the people of Newport flocked to see his demonstrations. Since he had read in "An historical account" that the lectures were popular throughout Europe, he decided to try them in Boston. Accordingly, the first formal lecture in America devoted wholly to electricity (Spencer's were on science and medicine) was advertised in the *Boston Evening Post* for August 24, 1747.[37]

> For the Entertainment
> of the Curious,
>
> There is to be seen at the House of Capt. John Williams, near the Golden Fleece in King-street, Boston, A Great Variety of curious Experiments of the most surprizing Effects of Electricity, wherein will be shewn the wonderful Phenomena of Electrical Attraction, Repulsion and flamific Force; particularly the new Method of electerising several Persons at the same Time, so that Fire shall dart from all Parts of their Bodies, as the same has lately been exhibited, to the Astonishment of the Curious in all Parts of Europe.
>
> Performed by William Claggett, Clock-maker, whose Business will not suffer him to make any long Stay here, and therefore should be glad those Gentlemen and Ladies whose Curiosities may excite them to behold those Wonders, would attend as soon as possible.
>
> N.B. These Experiments may be seen at any Time of the Day, a Company presenting, at Ten Shillings (Old Tenor) each Person.

Claggett also advertised in the *Boston Evening Post* on August 31 and September 7, 1747. On September 28,

---

[37] A survey of most of the lecturers on electricity in colonial Boston, reprinting a number of their advertisements, is given by William Northrop Morse, "Lectures on Electricity in Colonial Times," *New England Quarterly* VII (1934), 364–74.

Claggett's advertisement said that he had to leave for New-port within a few days and that Captain John Williams would continue the experiments after he left. Williams (at whose home Claggett had been lecturing) used Claggett's equipment[38] and was taught by Claggett. Williams' advertise-ments appeared in the *Boston Evening Post* for October 5, 19, 26, and November 2 and 16, 1747. Daniel King at Salem became a rival of Williams, advertising in the *Boston Evening Post* for October 12 and 19, 1747. The demonstra-tions by Claggett were undoubtedly extremely successful: it has even been written that he "received about £1500 in three weeks."[39]

In 1748, the vogue of the electrical demonstrations spread to New York and Charleston. Richard Brickell, another imitator of Claggett, advertised in the *New York Post-Boy* for May 2, 1748. Of greater interest is Samuel Dömjén,[40] "a very singular character" whom Franklin taught, probably in the spring of 1748. Dömjén's first advertisement in the *South Carolina Gazette* appeared October 31, 1748.

> The Subscriber having for many Years past in his Travels thro' Europe (from his native Country Transylvania) studied and made many wonderful experiments in ELECTRICITY, proposes to give Attendance at Mr. Blythe's Tavern in Broad-street, from the Hour of 3 to 5 in the Afternoon, on Wednes-day and Friday weekly during his stay in this Town (and when desired, will wait on Ladies and Gent. in their Houses) to shew the surprising Effects thereof. Each Person to see the same, to pay 20s who may also be *electrised* if they please, by Samuel Dömjén.

---

[38] *Boston Evening Post*, October 26, 1747.
[39] By the Reverend Arthur A. Ross, in an address delivered at Newport in 1838—quoted by Howard M. Chapin, "Was William Claggett, the clockmaker, an engraver?" Rhode Island Historical Society, *Collections*, XXII (1929), 42.
[40] There is a biographical note on Dömjén in Labaree, IV, 480.

Replying to an enquiry concerning Dömjén from Dr. John Lining, Franklin wrote that from Philadelphia, Dömjén "travelled thro' Maryland, Virginia, and North-Carolina to you."

> He thought it might be of service to him in his travels to know something of Electricity. I taught him the use of the tube; how to charge the Leyden phial, and some other experiments. He wrote to me from Charles-Town, that he had lived eight hundred miles upon Electricity, it had been meat, drink, and cloathing to him. His last letter to me was, I think, from Jamaica, desiring me to send the tubes you mention, to meet him, at the Havanah, from whence he expected to get a passage to La Vera Cruz; designed travelling over land through Mexico to Acapulco; thence to get a passage to Manilla, and so through China, India, Persia, and Turkey, home to his own country; proposing to support himself chiefly by Electricity. A strange project! But he was, as you observe, a very singular character.[41]

Dömjén, according to Franklin, gave lectures between Philadelphia and Charleston—but no trace of these has turned up.

3. KINNERSLEY'S TOURS, 1749–1753

The *Gentleman's Magazine* for January, 1750, published a short article entitled, "By a Number of Experiments, lately made in Philadelphia, several of the principal Properties of the Electrical Fire were demonstrated, and its effects shewn."[42] Although this article has been considered Benjamin Franklin's first separate published piece on electricity, I am able to show that it actually appeared nine months earlier in the *Maryland Gazette*. Also I am now able to offer proof of the perceptive suggestion of I. Bernard Cohen that the

[41] Labaree, V, 522.
[42] Pp. 34–35.

Gentleman's Magazine article is a copy of an early outline of the Reverend Ebenezer Kinnersley's lectures on electricty.[43]

Previously, it has been thought that Kinnersley's first lecture on electricity was advertised in the *Pennsylvania Gazette* for April 11, 1751. Actually he gave his lectures nearly two years before this. A series of advertisements and editorial notes in the May and June, 1749, issues of the *Maryland Gazette* show that Kinnersley was then lecturing in Annapolis. The probable reason for their not being previously noticed is that none of the notices give Kinnersley's name. There can be no mistake about their origin since they are practically identical with later advertisements known to be his. In addition, Kinnersley was in Annapolis at this time, for he was a guest at the Annapolis Tuesday Club on May 16 and June 13, 1749.[44]

Kinnersley's lectures are the joint product of Franklin and Kinnersley. In his *Memoirs,* Franklin points out that Kinnersley was the principal collaborator in his electrical experiments. Since Kinnersley lacked employment, Franklin encouraged him

> to undertake shewing the experiments for money, and drew up for him two lectures, in which the experiments were rang'd in such order, and accompanied with such explanations in such method, as that the foregoing should assist in comprehending the following. He procur'd an elegant apparatus for the purpose, in which all the little machines that I had roughly made for myself were nicely form'd by instrument-makers. His lectures were well attended and gave great Satisfaction; and after some time he went thro' the Colonies exhibiting them in every capital Town, and pick'd up some Money.[45]

---

[43] *Benjamin Franklin's Experiments,* p. 89.
[44] "Records of the Tuesday Club," pp. 135 and 138–39. MS. Maryland Historical Society.
[45] Farrand, pp. 380 and 382.

It cannot be positively known to what extent the first published outline was written, altered, or abridged by Kinnersley, but his influence is doubtlessly there. A survey of Kinnersley's advertisements shows that he constantly changed their order, rephrased some, and added others. As Kinnersley was an extremely careful, conscientious person, it is not likely that he would have begun his tour of the Southern Colonies until he had prepared every detail of his lectures and rehearsed them until they met high standards. Nevertheless, the syllabus always remained essentially the same, and, no doubt, it was essentially Franklin's.

Various writers[46] have puzzled why Franklin should have felt it necessary to write the lectures for the man who was, at his instigation, appointed Professor of English and Oratory at the College and Academy of Philadelphia. Although Kinnersley was already a well-known preacher and writer of Philadelphia, I believe that Franklin's action was natural. By his own account, Franklin had his house continually full with people who came to see his experiments. It is quite possible that Kinnersley (at the time when Franklin encouraged him to undertake showing the experiments for money) had rarely, if ever, given talks on them. Naturally, Franklin, who for months had been demonstrating experiments to his friends, would know better than Kinnersley how an audience could best be kept absorbed. In addition, his superior knowledge of the principles of electricity would better qualify him for arranging "the experiments in such order, and accompanied with such explanations in such method, as that the foregoing should assist in comprehending the following." Indeed, it is likely that Franklin's draft of Kinnersley's lectures set forth Franklin's single-fluid system of electricity in the most

---

[46] E.g., *Benjamin Franklin's Experiments*, p. 405.

thorough, systematic, and fascinating expression to that date.

Ebenezer Kinnersley was the greatest lecturer of colonial America. His lectures were popular for at least twenty-five years, and most of the lecturers on electricity after 1749 copied his experiments and manner of advertising. To a degree, Kinnersley's lectures may be taken as an indication of the colonists' interests; therefore, the reasons for the success of the lectures are worth investigating. Kinnersley usually advertised a syllabus of his experiments in newspapers and broadsides—no earlier lecturer issued a syllabus as an advertisement. This was a superior advertisement (at least while the experiments were new). The most important appeal was to the scientific curiosity of the people. Today, because of the departmentalization of knowledge, this might not be effective; it *was* in the eighteenth century. "Notice is . . . given to the Curious" began the advertisement. Kinnersley first demonstrated six properties of electricity. He was always eager to explain what he knew to those who were really interested (and perhaps he hoped to come across a brilliant suggestion): "Any gentleman proposing a new experiment may have it try'd at a vacant time; and the reasons as far as hitherto known, of every operation, will be given at leisure to curious enquirers."

Kinnersley appealed to the patriotism of his audience: "a course of experiments on the newly discovered electrical fire: containing not only those that have been made and published in Europe, but a number of new ones lately made in Philadelphia; by which several of the principal properties of this wonderful fire are demonstrated." He also appealed to their superstitions, fears, and sense of the marvelous: "A leaf of the most weighty of metals, suspended in the air, as is said of Mahomet's Tomb," and "An artificial spider, animated by electrical fire acting like a live one, and endeavouring to catch a fly." Kinnersley even had a hypothesis explaining the solar system—"A small globe revolving around a larger, as the earth does around the sun."[47] And small animals could be killed by electricity "instantaneously."

There was a social, and perhaps romantic, lure: "Spirits kindled by fire darting from a lady's eyes (without a metaphor)"; "The salute [kiss] repulsed by the ladies fire." The price of the tickets encouraged bringing a lady: "The price of a ticket to admit a gentleman and a lady, seven shillings and six pence; a single person five shillings."

The lectures were a rare opportunity to be entertained, amused, taught, and perhaps frightened. More important than being a social occasion, they were a democratic institution. Before the rise of the popular lecturers, science was a fashionable and fairly exclusive club. An interest in science was one of the indications of a cultivated gentleman. The roll call of colonial American scientists contains few who were not leaders in colonial American society. In the case of the exceptions, like John Bartram, their interest and ability in science was alone enough to make them well-known to the cultivated eighteenth century gentleman. But at the popular

---

[47] In his manuscript "A Course of Experiments on the Newly Discover'd Electrical Fire, 1752," printed by I. Bernard Cohen in *Benjamin Franklin's Experiments,* Kinnersley suggests two hypotheses explaining the solar system (pp. 419–20). According to the first, the "mutual Repulsion of electrified Bodies" is "a probable Cause of the Planets keeping their due Distances from each other, & from the Sun in the Center." But the "more probable" hypothesis depends upon the attraction of bodies. The sun, "highly electrified," would attract the planets, but "let us suppose the Creator to bowl [the planet] as it were from his forming-finishing hand in such a Direction & with such a projectile Force, as might be sufficient to counter-ballance the strong attraction of the electrified Sun & then the Planet will rowl on thro' the unresisting Aether in a regular Orbit, & perform perpetual Revolutions round its Center."

lectures, the peasants and craftsmen[48] as well as the aristocracy (who, to be sure, often arranged for private demonstrations) were welcome. The lectures supplied an opportunity for education and helped to create a desire for knowledge, resulting, in part, in the nineteenth century lyceum movement.

Perhaps the most fascinating and significant single item in the syllabus of experiments is: "Various representations of lightning, the causes and effects of which will be explained by a more probable hypothesis than has hitherto appeared; and some useful instructions given how to avoid the danger of it." Throughout the ages scientists had suspected that lightning and electricity might be the same, and as more powerful electric sparks were created in the first half of the eighteenth century, the suspicion grew. The author of "An historic account" had speculated on the identity of lightning and electricity, but no previous experimenter had marshalled the experiments, the analogies, and fully detailed reasoning behind his conviction. Franklin was the first to give a full-dress scientific hypothesis of the identification of lightning and electricity. He did this in a letter "wrote for Mr. Kinnersley," a copy of which, dated April 29, 1749, was sent to Dr. John Mitchel.[49] Less than two weeks later, Kinnersley advertised that he could explain the causes and effects of lightning by a more probable hypothesis than "has hitherto appeared." In Annapolis, May 15, 1749, Kinnersley made the first public argument for the identification of lightning and electricity.

---

[48] Carl Bridenbaugh, *The Colonial Craftsman* (New York, 1950), p. 169.

[49] Labaree, III, 365, assigns the addressee as John Mitchel, not mentioning Franklin's account in the *Memoirs*, "One Paper which I wrote for Mr. Kinnersley, on the Sameness of Lightning with Electricity, I sent to Dr. Mitchel . . :" Farrand, p. 382.

This, then, was the course of experiments that Kinnersley advertised in the *Maryland Gazette* for May 10, 17, and 24, 1749, the experiments that Franklin had drawn up, and that Kinnersley and others were to continue giving throughout America for at least the next quarter century.

NOTICE is hereby given to the Curious,

That at the House where Mr. *Walter Dulany* lately lived, in *Annapolis,* will be exhibited from Day to Day (the Weather being fair) for the space of a Fortnight, a Course of Experiments on the newly discovered ELECTRICAL FIRE: containing not only those that have been made and published in *Europe,* but a Number of new ones lately made in *Philadelphia;* by which several of the principal Properties of this wonderful *Fire* are demonstrated; *viz.*

That it is a real *Element,* intimately united with all other Matter, from whence it is *collected* by the Tube, or Sphere, and not *created* by the Friction.

That tho' it will fire inflammable Bodies, itself has no sensible Heat.

That it doth not, like common Matter, take up any perceptible Time in passing thro' great Portions of Space.

That Bodies replete with this Fire strongly attract such as have less of it, and repel such as have an equal Quantity.

That it will live in Water, a River not being sufficient to quench the smallest Spark of it.

That contrary to other Matter, it is more strongly attracted by slender sharp Points, than by solid blunt Bodies, &c &c.

Among other curious Particulars, will be shewn, a Representation of the Sensitive Plant.

A small Globe revolving round a larger, as the Earth does round the Sun.

A Representation of the seven Planets, shewing a probable Cause of their keeping at a Distance.

An artificial Spider, animated by Electrical Fire, acting like a live one, and endeavouring to catch a Fly.

A Leaf of the most weighty of Metals, suspended in the Air, as is said of Mahomet's Tomb.

A Perpetual shower of Sand, which rises again as fast as it falls.

Various Representations of Lightning, the Cause and Effects of which will be explained by a more probable Hypothesis than has hitherto appeared; and some useful Instructions given how to avoid the Danger of it.

The Force of the Electrical Spark, making a fair hole thro' a Quire of Paper.

Small Animals killed by it Instantaneously.

Spirits kindled by Fire darting from a Lady's Eyes (without a Metaphor).

Spirits of Wine also kindled by a Spark after it has passed thro' ten Foot of Water. Also by Fire issuing out of a cold Egg.

An extinguished Candle lighted again by a Flame issuing out of cold Iron.

An Electrical Mine Sprung.

The amazing Force and Swiftness of the Electrical Fire in passing thro' a Number of Bodies at the same Instant.

A Piece of Money drawn out of a Persons Mouth in spite of his Teeth, yet without touching it, or offering him the least Violence.

The Salute repuls'd by the Ladies Fire.

Eight musical Bells rung by an electrisied Phial. Also by an electrisied Picture.

A Battery of eleven Guns discharged by Fire issuing out of a Mans Finger.

In order that different Companies may not interfere with, and incommode each other, Tickets will be given out for each Exhibition, expressing the Time, &c.

The Price of a Ticket, to admit a Gentleman and a Lady, Seven Shillings and six pence; a single Person Five Shillings. The first Exhibition will be on Monday the 15th Instant if the

Weather be fair, and Tickets may be had at the Dwelling House of Mr. *John Lomas*, in *Annapolis*.

Any Gentlemen proposing a new Experiment may have it try'd at a vacant Time; and the Reasons, as far as hitherto known, of every Operation, will be given at Leisure to curious Enquirers, by

Their humble Servant,

The Operator.[50]

The electrical lecturers in America before Kinnersley contented themselves with imitating European achievements. Kinnersley's lectures were original. He expounded and proved by experiments the Franklinian system of electricity; electricity was not created by friction, but collected from matter; an analysis of the Leyden jar proved the superiority of Franklin's single-fluid theory of electricity; and, of course, Kinnersley first publicly hypothesized and (later) demonstrated the electrical nature of lightning.[51]

Not all his experiments, however, were original. Among the "most curious' 'experiments "made and published in Europe" that Kinnersley adopted were the electrical kiss (published in the *Gentleman's Magazine* article—though Franklin and Kinnersley found how to increase its force "vastly");[52] the experiment that extracted "a crown piece from between a man's teeth, in spite of all his endeavours to hold it"; the experiment showing that electricity does not take up "any perceptible time in passing thro' great Portions of Space"; the experiment setting spirits of wine on fire; and, of course, the standard experiment that Greenwood, Spencer, and Claggett had before all demonstrated in America, "That

---

[50] *Maryland Gazette,* May 10, 1749.

[51] Labaree, III, 129–30, 157–64, and 365–72.

[52] "An historical account," p. 196a ; Labaree, III, 133.

Bodies replete with this Fire strongly attract such as have less of it, and repel such as have an equal Quantity."[53]

Kinnersley's lectures were a resounding success: Jonas Green, the editor of the *Maryland Gazette*, inserted in his edition of May 31, 1749:

> We hear, that the gentleman who exhibits the electrical experiments, designs, before he leaves this place (which will be in a few days), to fire spirits of wine, and discharge his battery of eleven guns, by an electrical spark, that shall first pass thro' the water from Mr. Hill's point to Mr. Carroll's; which is supposed to be about a quarter of a mile.

And in the *Maryland Gazette* for June14, 1749, Green tells the outcome of the experiment:

> On Friday last, the gentleman who has exhibited the electrical experiments in town, removed his machine over to the south side of our creek; and having set some spirits of wine, in a small vessel, on a table on the north side, he caused a spark of electrical fire to dart across in an instant, through 200 yards of water, which set the spirits in a blaze the first attempt, and several times afterwards; and discharged a battery of eleven guns, to the surprise and great satisfaction of the spectators. His experiments are all of them very curious and entertaining, and have given general satisfaction to all who have seen them here. He intends the first opportunity for Norfolk, and other parts of Virginia.

Kinnersley probably left for Virginia in the latter part of June, 1749. Thus far no Virginia records have turned up that positively prove he lectured there. The only likely place to find a record of his presence would be in the *Virginia Gazette*. Although contemporary evidence indicates that the *Gazette* was published until sometime in 1750, there are no extant copies of it for 1749 or 1750. But in view of Kinners-

---

[53] "An historical account," pp. 196a and 193a ; and the notices of Claggett's progress in electricity above.

ley's expressed intention to go to Virginia and the fact that no other lecturer was active at this time,[54] the   ng news item, which appeared in the *Maryland*   for October 18, 1749, is probably about Kinnersley:

Williamsburg, August 31.

We have receiv'd the following Certificate from Suffolk:

Suffolk, August 18, 1749.

The gentleman who has been entertaining us with a Course of very curious Electrical Experiments has also applied the Electrical Fire to the human frame, with remarkable and speedy success, in curing the tooth ache, pains in the head, deafness, pains in the limbs, which had been so violent as to take away the use of them, pain in the stomach, swelling of the spleen, sprains, relaxation of the nerves, &c. The most remarkable are the two following instances, *viz*.

One Samuel Miller, who for three years past could not lift his hand above his head without putting his shoulder out of joint, by a few applications of the electrical fire has met with a perfect cure.

An negro boy, about sixteen years of age, who had always been so deaf as scarcely to hear the loudest sounds, has by the same means been brought to hear, when spoke to in a common tone of voice.

We the subscribers thought proper to give this information to the public, that others, who may have the opportunity, might be encouraged to make further trial of this wonderful remedy.

Robert Brown,	William Webb,	Robert Cook,
David Meade,	John Watson,	John Marlow,
Lemuel Riddeck,	John Wright,	Alex. Cairnes.[55]

[54] The next lecturer on electricity in America, Lewis Evans, seems not to have begun before 1751.

[55] This was evidently reprinted from the *Virginia Gazette* of August 31. It was also reprinted by the *Pennsylvania Journal*, December 5, 1749, and the *Boston Evening Post*, January 1, 1750. It is interesting to note that popular interest in electricity was greatest in the areas where the lecturers had been active.

The only Southern newspaper published at this time that ha known extant copies is the *South Carolina Gazette*. A survey his newspaper reveals that Kinnersley did not go to Charleston: perhaps because he wanted to be back in Philadelphia by winter, or perhaps because Samuel Dömjén had recently lectured there. The *South Carolina Gazette* for May 28, 1750, printed (probably from the *Gentleman's Magazine*)[56] the syllabus of experiments for Kinnersley's lectures; therefore, it seems unlikely that the people of Charleston had seen his lectures. After his tour through Maryland and Virginia, Kinnersley probably returned to Philadelphia for the winter.

On February 4, 1751, Franklin wrote to Collinson, telling him of the experiments that he and Kinnersley had just performed. Kinnersley "has apply'd my horizontal self-moving Wheel with Success, to the playing of Tunes on Chimes, which it does very prettily."[57] Kinnersley advertised in the *Pennsylvania Gazette* for April 11 and 18, and May 2, 1751. In addition to what he had printed in the *Maryland Gazette* concerning lightning—"Various Representations of Lightning, the Cause and Effects of which will be explained by a more probable Hypothesis than has hitherto appeared, and some useful Instructions given how to avoid the Danger of it"—Kinnersley adds, "How to secure Houses, Ships, &c. from being hurt by its destructive Violence." In these lectures Kinnersley showed the public the first demonstrations of the lightning rod. Franklin had written in "Opinions and Conjectures":

> Now if the Fire of Electricity, and that of Lightning, be the same; . . . may not the Knowledge of this Power of Points be of Use to Mankind; in preserving Houses, Churches,

[56] Minor textual evidences support this reasoning.
[57] Labaree, IV, 12.

Ships &c. from the Stroke of Lightning; by Directing us to fix
on the highest Parts of those Edifices upright Rods of Iron,
made sharp as a Needle and gilt to prevent Rusting, and from
the Foot of those Rods a Wire down the outside of the Building into the Ground; or down round one of the Shrouds of
a Ship and down her Side, till it reach'd the Water?[58]

This was the theory. To illustrate the practice, Kinnersley
made several miniature houses and ships: the ones that did
not have lightning-rods were burst asunder by a small stroke
of electricity, and perhaps combustible material in them was
set on fire; the ones that had lightning rods carried the spark
of electricity safely through them.[59]

Franklin had proposed in paragraph 21 of "Opinions and
Conjectures" (published in the spring of 1751 in his *Experiments and Observations on Electricity*), his famous sentry-
box experiment, which would prove the identity of lightning
and electricity.[60] On May 10, 1752, Dalibard, a French
scientist, following Franklin's instructions, joyously verified
the hypothesis.[61] News of Dalibard's test did not reach
America, however, until after Franklin had made his famous
kite experiment. But Kinnersley had been demonstrating the
"probable hypothesis" of the identity of lightning and
electricity since May 15, 1749.

In September, 1751, Kinnersley set out on his tour of the

---

[58] Labaree, IV, 18–19. Although dated 1749 in *Experiments and
Observations,* Labaree *et al.* believe that Franklin did not write this
until July 29, 1750. *Ibid.,* p. 9.

[59] These experiments were performed with gadgets similar to those
described in I. Bernard Cohen, *Some Early Tools of American
Science* (Cambridge, Massachusetts, 1950). See Nos. 17—19, Profile
of a House, Steeple with Lightning Rod, and Thunder House, pp.
161–62. There are photographs of these ingenious contrivances
following p. 154.

[60] Labaree, IV, 19–20.

[61] Labaree, IV, 302 and 360.

northern colonies with a letter of introduction to James Bowdoin given him by Franklin:

September 5, 1751

As you are curious in electricity, I take the freedom of introducing to you, my friend Mr. Kinnersley, who visits Boston with a complete apparatus for experimental lectures on that subject. He has given great satisfaction to all that have heard him here, and I believe you will be pleased with his performance. He is quite a stranger in Boston; and, as you will find him a sensible, worthy man, I hope he will be favored with your countenance, and the encouragement which that must procure him among your friends.[62]

Kinnersley had broadsides printed in Boston and began lecturing in Faneuil Hall in September.[63] He advertised in the *Boston Evening Post* for October 7, November 4 and 18, 1751, and January 13 and 20, 1752. The length of Kinnersley's stay in Boston (five months), and Bowdoin's letter to Franklin, both attest to Kinnersley's popularity:

The Experiments Mr. Kennersley has exhibited here, have been greatly pleasing to all sorts of people, that have seen them; and I hope by the time he returns to Philadelphia, his Tour this way will turn to good account. His experiments are very curious, and I think, prove most effectually your doctrine of Electricity."[64]

Reverend Andrew Eliot, who disapproved of the "modern theatre" and was not a student of science, attended Kinnersley's lectures and seemingly accepted his arguments. John Perkins also commented that Kinnersley was "well-receiv'd," and that he has seen the "entertaining" experiments.[65]

---

[62] *Ibid.*, pp. 191–92.

[63] Although I have not been able to locate a copy of this broadside, its existence in 1905 was recorded in "Lectures on Electricity in 1751," *Electrical Review* for May 13, 1905, p. 783.

[64] Bowdoin's letter is dated December 21, 1751. Labaree, IV, 216.

[65] Clifford K. Shipton, *Biographical Sketches of Those Who Attended Harvard College, 1736–1740* (series title: *Sibley's Harvard Graduates,* Vol. X) (Boston, 1958), p. 132. Labaree, IV, 267–68.

In addition to lecturing, Kinnersley performed, with James Bowdoin, a number of experiments, the results of which were communicated in Bowdoin's letter to Franklin, December 21, 1751, and in Kinnersley's letter to Franklin, dated Boston, February 3, 1752. Bowdoin's letter concerns "the communication of magnetism to needles by electricity," and offers an explanation of the "crooked Direction of lightning."[66] Kinnersley immediately incorporated these latest discoveries into his lectures: at the end of his October 7 advertisement, he added, "N.B. It has lately been discovered, that the Magnetic Vertue may be given to a Needle, and that Gun-Powder may be fired immediately by the Electric Spark." Kinnersley's letter to Franklin told of his independent rediscovery of Dufay's vitreous and resinous electricity. Franklin's two replies to Kinnersley explained the difference as merely being positive and negative–an aspect of Franklin's single-fluid theory. Kinnersley's letter to Franklin, printed in *Supplemental Experiments and Observations on Electricity, Part II* (London, 1753), was his first published writing on electricity (exclusive of advertisements) and brought Kinnersley his first notice outside the colonies.[67]

Early in March, Kinnersley went to Newport, Rhode Island, where he published a broadside on March 16, 1752.[68] He evidently stayed in Newport until May 11. Kinnersley was extraordinarily successful in meeting the religious prejudice of his audience–an audience that was convinced that lightning was God's special providence and that light-

[66] Labaree, IV, 216–21.

[67] *Ibid.*, pp. 256–59, 263–65, 269, and 275–76. Collinson, who had received Kinnersley's letter for printing from Franklin, wrote on July 7, 1752, "It's likely our Friend Kennersly may add some others, under thy Direction." *Ibid.*, p. 333.

[68] This is reproduced in Bern Dibner, *Early Electrical Machines* (Norwalk, Connecticut, 1957), p. 35.

ning was not electricity (whatever that was). The first time that Kinnersley demonstrated a means (the lightning rod) to prevent the harmful effect of a stroke of lightning, he also included a justification, religious and secular, for experimenting with electricity: "As the knowledge of Nature tends to enlarge the human Mind, and give us more noble, more grand and exalted ideas of the Author of Nature, and if well pursu'd seldom fails producing something *useful* to man, 'tis hoped these Lectures may be thought worthy of Regard and Encouragement."[69] Fortunately, an account of a typical reaction to Kinnersley's lectures is preserved:

It was, I confess, with no small Degree of Prejudice that I first attended these *Lectures,* but I was determin'd to see and judge for myself, and it was with no small Satisfaction that I found myself agreeably disappointed; for though I thought any Endeavours to explain the Cause of Lightning, which had puzzled and perplex'd the Philosophy of every Age, idle and vain; and any Attempt to avoid so subtile a Fire, mere Presumption; the Truth of this Gentleman's Hypothesis, appear'd in so glaring a Light, and with such undeniable Evidence, that all my former pre-conceiv'd Notions of Thunder and Lightning, tho' borrow'd from the most sagacious Philosophers, together with my Prejudices, immediately vanish'd;—all the Accounts of the celebrated Naturalists appear'd (as they really were,) conjectural and chimerical; the Wisdom of Providence, having reserv'd the Discovery of that wonderful *Phaenomenon,* which has been a Mystery, wrapp'd up in Clouds and think Darkness ever since it's first Appearance, to the present Age, and entirely to the Improvements made on the *Electric Fire,* by ingenious *Americans.*[70]

Kinnersley was lecturing in a time when after every

---

[69] *Pennsylvania Gazette,* April 11, 1751.
[70] *New York Gazette,* June 1, 1752. See Frontispiece.

unusual display of natural phenomena a fresh flood of sermons appeared, claiming that the occurrence was God's warning to a wicked mankind. The scientists' attempts to understand and control lightning seemed to deny God's providence, to make Him, somehow, less powerful. That Kinnersley was able to introduce lightning rods without arousing strong protests marks him an extraordinarily judicious person. Three years later, Dr. John Lining caused a controversy with his experiments in South Carolina, and the charge of atheistical presumption was leveled against those who tried to introduce lightning rods until well after the beginning of the nineteenth century—just as evolution was opposed until well into the twentieth.[71] But Kinnersley was an ideal person to popularize the lightning rod, for he was obviously and undeniably quite religious. The Newport letter writer quoted above said:

> . . . his *Apparatus,* is very beautiful and well adapted to shew every Experiment to Advantage, in which he has happily succeeded in *New England,* to universal Satisfaction; for all his Exhibitions are perform'd with an Elegancy peculiar to himself, and the Whole is improv'd in a Manner answerable to, and becoming, the highest Christian Character; for he endeavours to make this new Branch of *Natural Philosophy,* subservient to the true Intent of all Knowledge, both natural and reveal'd, *viz.* to lead us to the first Cause by refining, enlarging and exalting our Ideas of the great Author and God of Nature; and who, therefore, but the Man that is Fool enough to say in his Heart, *there is no God,* wou'd think such

---

[71] I. Bernard Cohen has written a brilliant essay on this subject, "Prejudice against the Introduction of Lightning Rods," *Journal of the Franklin Institute,* CCLIII (1952), 393–440. Unfortunately, he did not include the earliest examples of opposition to the lightning rod—that encountered by Kinnersley, reflected above, and the vigorous prejudice Dr. John Lining met: *South Carolina Gazette,* July 30, 1753, and July 31, 1755.

Lectures unworthy of his highest Regard, or refuse to attend them

An example of Kinnersley's use of religion in his lectures occurs near the end of the first lecture. After speculating on the forces that keep the solar system from obeying the law of gravity and crashing together, he says:

> But if neither of these Hypotheses shou'd be true, there may notwithstanding be somewhat instructive in them. For by whatsoever natural Causes these glorious suspended Worlds are kept asunder in opposition to the great Force of mutual Gravity, which tends to bring them together, that Cause is in the Hands of the great Maker & Governour of the Universe. Shou'd he then for the Punishment of our Sins decree in his Anger to withdraw it, which Mercy forbid! all the Planets & their Satellites, all the massy Globes of this System wou'd rush suddenly together, dash each other to pieces, and form one mighty ruin.[72]

From Newport, Kinnersley went to New York, where his first advertisements appeared on May 18, 1752, in the *New York Mercury* and the *New York Gazette and Weekly Post-Boy*. They were repeated in the latter newspaper on May 25, June 1 and 15, and July 6 and 20. Kinnersley's advertisement on the front page of the *New York Gazette* for June 1, 1752 (reproduced herein as the frontispiece) is the best single illustration of the appeal of his lectures and of their effect upon the people. On June 13, 1752, James Alexander wrote to Cadwalader Colden, "I doubt not you have Seen the advertisement of Mr. Kinnerslys Lectures on Electricity— I have been to see both, and I assure you he performs them Extremely well being a Master of words as well as of the Experiments."[73] And Franklin wrote to Colden on September 14, "I am sorry you could not see Mr. Kinnersley's Lectures;

---

[72] *Benjamin Franklin's Experiments*, p. 421.
[73] *The Colden Papers*, IV (for 1920), 336.

they would have pleas'd you."[74] Kinnersley's notice for July 20 said that the "Course of Experiments and Lectures on Electricity will be continued here no longer than this Week."

Kinnersley probably returned to Philadelphia in August—nearly a year after he set out on his tour of the northern colonies. He had spent over five months in Boston, well over two in Newport, and almost three in New York. Back in Philadelphia, Kinnersley advertised in the *Pennsylvania Gazette* for September 14 and 28, 1752. In the issue for October 19, 1752, Franklin first made public his famous kite experiment, proving that lightning and electricity are the same. Across the bottom of that page of the *Pennsylvania Gazette* runs Kinnersley's striking notice, "The Lectures and Experiments on Electricity at the State-House are intended to be repeated but once more: The first Lecture to be on Monday next, the Weather being suitable, otherwise the first fair dry Day after."

In the fall of 1752, Kinnersley, escaping Philadelphia's bitter winter, left for the West Indies. He lectured on electricity there, for we have his broadside dated St. John's, Antigua, April 25, 1753.[75] On April 12, 1753, Franklin wrote to James Bowdoin, described glass jars coated with leaf tin, and said, "I had not Conveniency to coat them for you, and feared to trust anybody else, Mr. Kinnersley being abroad in the W Indies."[76] Although Philadelphia's craftsmen were probably the best in the colonies,[77] Franklin evidently felt

---

[74] Labaree, IV, 355.

[75] Facsimile in *Benjamin Franklin's Experiments,* facing p. 406. This was also reprinted in full by Worthington C. Ford, "New Light on Franklin's Electrical Experiments," *Nation,* LXXXVI (January 23, 1908), 85–86.

[76] Labaree, IV, 462.

[77] Carl and Jessica Bridenbaugh, *Rebels and Gentlemen* (New York, 1942), p. 320.

that they had to be carefully supervised if they were to produce the exact forms desired. There is little doubt that Kinnersley's apparatus was, from 1749 to his death in 1778, the best in the colonies. Franklin wrote in his *Memoirs* that Kinnersley "procur'd an elegant apparatus . . . in which all the little machines that I had roughly made for myself were nicely form'd by instrument-makers."[78] And David Rittenhouse, a competent judge, said of Kinnersley's instruments in 1778 that they were "perhaps equal to any apparatus of the kind in the world."[79]

While Kinnersley was in the West Indies, he received a letter from Franklin, asking if he would be interested in the position of Master of the English School of the Philadelphia Academy. Kinnersley was. He returned in the middle of June, 1753. William Franklin, June 28, wrote his father that Kinnersley had returned the previous week, discovered nothing new in electricity, and cleared about £200 sterling on his trip.[80] Ebenezer Kinnersley had lectured on electricity throughout the colonies and in the West Indies for over four years, from the spring of 1749 to the summer of 1753.

4.   FRANKLIN AND KINNERSLEY: THE RUMOR

The neurotic dissatisfaction on the part of some individuals with the actual state of things has leveled the charge that Shakespeare didn't write Shakespeare's plays and that Franklin stole the Franklinian system of electricity from Kinnersley. Since this charge has been repeated by many cursory and quackish students of Franklin, it seems that a

---

[78] Farrand, p. 381.
[79] Minutes of the Trustees, University of Pennsylvania, December 15, 1778. Book I, p. 117. Archives, University of Pennsylvania.
[80] Labaree, IV, 513–14.

biography of Kinnersley should be the place to squash it. The record will show that the charge was first made public in 1758 by a political enemy of Franklin, attempting, no doubt, to discredit him. There exists a possibility, however, that the charge reflected a rumor current in colonial America.

By 1752, when Kinnersley returned to Philadelphia from his tours of the American colonies, he was the most widely known electrical theorist and experimenter in America. For three years he had been lecturing on the Franklinian system of electricity, hypothesizing that lightning and electricity were the same. Credit for this startling theory and for the demonstrations (since at least April, 1751) of lightning rods was probably, by the masses, given to Kinnersley. Then, in the summer of 1752, came the news that Franklin's hypothesis had been confirmed by Dalibard. Franklin's name now came before the people in connection with electricity for the first time. As Franklin's reputation in electricity grew, it seems possible that there were some people who thought that Kinnersley really deserved the credit.

It was in the October, 1758, issue of the *American Magazine,* in an unsigned article by William Smith, "Account of the College and Academy of Philadelphia,"[81] that Franklin was first accused in print of stealing Kinnersley's theories:

> [Kinnersley] is well qualified for his profession; and has moreover great merit with the learned world in being the chief inventor . . . of the electrical apparatus, as well as author of a considerable part of those discoveries in electricity, published by Mr. Franklin to whom he communicated them. Indeed Mr. Franklin himself mentions his name with honor, tho' he has not been careful enough to distinguish between their particular discoveries. This, perhaps he may have thought

[81] I (1758), 639.

needless, as they were known to act in concert, But tho' that circumstance was known here, it was not so in the remote parts of the world to which the fame of these discoveries have extended.

The Reverend William Smith, Provost of the Philadelphia College and Academy, was in a position to know. But by this time, he was a political enemy of Franklin.

Kinnersley, Professor of English and Oratory at the Philadelphia College and Academy, wrote a letter refuting Smith, who, as Provost, was his immediate superior. Kinnersley's letter, published in the *Pennsylvania Gazette,* November 30, 1758, evaluates the contributions of the various performers to the "Philadelphia Experiments."

To the Author of the Account of the College and Academy of Philadelphia, published in the *American Magazine* for October, 1758.

Sir,

I was very much surprised and concerned to see the Account you have been pleased to give of my electrical Discoveries, in page 639 of the *American Magazine.* If you did it with a view to procure me esteem in the learned world, I should have been abundantly more obliged to you, had it been done, so as to have no tendency to depreciate the merit of the ingenious and worthy Mr. Franklin, in the many curious and justly celebrated discoveries he has made in electricity. Had you said that, being honoured with Mr. Franklin's intimacy, I was often with him when he was making experiments, and that new discoveries were sometimes made when we were together, and at other times some were made by myself at home, and communicated to Mr. Franklin, this would have been really true, though it is what I never desired to have published. But to say, 'That I am the author of a considerable part of those discoveries in electricity, published by Mr. Franklin'; the expression, from whomsoever you might have the intelligence, appears too strong; it may be understood to comprehend more than is strictly true, and therefore I thought myself obliged to take this public notice of it. If you will please, Sir, to examine what Mr. Franklin had published on electricity, I think you will no where find that he appropriates to himself the honour of any one discovery; but is so complaisant to his electrical friends, as always to say, in the plural number, *we* have found out, or, *we* discovered, &c. As to his not being careful to distinguish between the particular discoveries of each; this perhaps was not always practicable; it being sometimes impossible to recollect in whose breast the thought first took rise, that led to a series of experiments, which at length issued in some unexpected important discovery. But had it been always practicable to distinguish between the particular discoveries of each, it was altogether unnecessary; as, I believe, none of Mr. Franklin's electrical friends had the least thought of ever appearing as competitors for any of the honours that they have beheld, with pleasure, bestowed on him, and to which he has an undoubted right, preferable to the united merit of all the electricians in America, and, perhaps, in all the World.

I am, Sir, Your most obedient Servant,

Ebenezer Kinnersley

Kinnersley's letter probably led Franklin to try to credit each of his fellow experimenters with their contributions. He made these notes in his own copy of the 1751 edition and published many of the credits in the fourth English edition of *Experiments and Observations*. But Franklin's notes of credit did little to stop the rumor. Jonathan Boucher wrote that he often heard that Franklin stole the credit for Kinnersley's discoveries:

Franklin's enemies, however bitter, have seldom been found so wanting in truth and justice as to deny him great merit in his philosophical character: it was in Philadelphia chiefly, if not solely, and by his friends, that he was charged with having stolen from an Irish gentleman, of the name of Kinnersley, many of his useful discoveries respecting electricity. How truly he was, or was not, the discoverer of the electrical nature of lightning, I cannot, amid such a variety of contradictory evidence, take upon me to determine; but common justice requires that I should acknowledge, that, in his day, no man contributed more to excite and foster a spirit for investigation and experiment; and that he first effectually practised, what Lord Verulam first conceived and recommended, *viz,* the stripping philosophy of her uncouth scholastic garb and rendering her the companion and friend of all orders of men.

Tender and cautious as I am, and ought to be, of bringing a charge of plagiarism against a man who can no longer vindicate himself, I cannot help observing, that though I certainly have often heard the allegation used against Dr. Franklin in America, and though it was set down as it now stands in this place soon after my hearing it in Philadelphia, from a gentleman who was well acquainted with both the parties; it must strike everyone as amounting almost to a direct refutation of the charge, that Kinnersley does not appear to have claimed any share in a discovery to which Dr. Franklin publicly avowed his own claim, but this successful plagiarism, admitting it to have been one, is not the only instance of its kind imputed to the Doctor, . . .[82]

Alexander Graydon, in his autobiography, *Memoirs of a Life, Chiefly Passed in Pennsylvania,* recalled his former teacher, the Reverend Ebenezer Kinnersley, as a "large, venerable looking man, who, whether truly or not, has been said to have had a share in certain discoveries in that science of which Doctor Franklin received the whole credit."[83] And James Jones Wilmer revealed that he knew the rumor but discredited it:

In his experiments, it is said, he was assisted by the Rev. Ebenezer Kinnersley, Professor. . . . He [Franklin] undoubt-

---

[82] Jonathan Boucher, *A View of the Causes and Consequences of the American Revolution* (London, 1797), pp. 438–39.
[83] (Harrisburgh, 1811), p. 16.

edly improved by the experience of this ingenious gentleman; but his own sagacious and active mind led him on to discoveries that will immortalize his name.[84]

The last author who probably had enough contact with mid-eighteenth century America to have received his account not only from secondary sources was William Barton. He wrote of Kinnersley:

> This venerable and worthy man, who was a clergyman of the Baptist Church, was a very eminent Electrician. In this branch of philosophy, he was an able lecturer and ingenious experimentalist; and perhaps io no person—at least in America—were his contemporaries more indebted, than to him, for the light which he shed, at a very early day, on this interesting and pleasing science.[85]

Barton's statement is true only if he is speaking of spreading knowledge among the people. Kinnersley certainly knew that Franklin was his master in electricity. His letters to Franklin invariably reveal the relationship of a gifted student to his teacher; typical is his statement, "I should be glad to see these phaenomena better accounted for by your superior and more penetrating genius."[86]

There is no doubt that their friendship continued throughout Kinnersley's life. After Franklin was disgracefully handled before the Privy Council, Kinnersley, in a dramatic expression of colonial hostility toward England, burned the effigies of his interrogator Alexander Wedderburn and the Royal Governor of Massachusetts, Thomas Hutchinson, by electric fire before an enraged crowd of Philadelphians.[87]

---

[84] James Jones Wilmer, *Memoirs of the Late Dr. Benjamin Franklin* . . . (London, 1790), pp. 10–11.

[85] William Barton, *Memoirs of David Rittenhouse* (Philadelphia, 1813), p. 155.

[86] *Benjamin Franklin's Experiments*, p. 350.

[87] *Pennsylvania Gazette*, May 4, 1774.

And Franklin expressed concern for Kinnersley when the latter was ill in 1772.[88]

If Kinnersley is recognized as the greatest popularizer in America of the wonders of electricity and the usefulness of lightning rods, and if his own important and original contributions to the study of electricity are remembered, then he has all of the just credit in electricity to which he seems entitled. The new theory and the boldest imaginative reasoning on electricity were Franklin's. Kinnersley closed his most important letter to Franklin with these words:

And now, Sir, I most heartily congratulate you on the pleasure you must have in finding your great and well-grounded expectations so far fulfilled. May this method of security from the destructive violence of one of the most awful powers of nature, meet with such further success, as to induce every good and grateful heart to bless God for the important discovery! May the benefit thereof be diffused over the whole globe! May it extend to the latest posterity of mankind, and make the name of FRANKLIN, like that of *NEWTON, immortal.*[89].

---

[88] Albert Henry Smyth, ed., *The Writings of Benjamin Franklin* (New York, 1905–1907), V, 396.
[89] *Benjamin Franklin's Experiments,* p. 358.

III Teacher and Scientist, 1753-1778

ON JULY 10, 1753, at a meeting of the Trustees of the Philadelphia Academy and Charitable School:

> Mr. Peters informed the Trustees, that in pursuance of their Resolution of providing a new Master for the English School, Mr. Franklin had sometime since wrote to Mr. Ebenezer Kinnersley, then in the West Indies to know if that Place would be agreeable to him, and that Mr. Kinnersley was now come over and had signified his Willingness to accept thereof, if the Trustees approve of him.
>
> The Trustees present, having express'd their Approbation of Mr. Kinnersley, thought proper to send for Mr. Dove and acquaint him that they had provided a new Master for the said School pursuant to their Intention signified to him some Months ago; who, thereupon, declared he would attend the School no longer. Mr. Kinnersley being then sent for, accepted the Charge of the said School for one Year. His Salery to be One Hundred and fifty Pounds per Annum.[1]

Thus the Reverend Ebenezer Kinnersley, then approaching forty-two years of age, began another career through the influence of his friend, Benjamin Franklin.

Kinnersley relegated his scientific pursuits to a part-time interest, but one that he pursued as fully as his time permitted. On July 23, 1753, Franklin wrote to his son William that he was glad to hear that William had taken full notes of the appearance of Trumble's house, which had been struck

---

[1] Minutes of the Trustees, University of Pennsylvania, I, 32–33. Archives, University of Pennsylvania. Hereafter cited as Minutes.

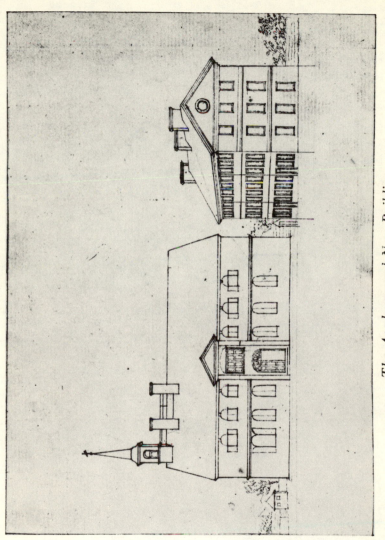

The Academy and New Building

by lightning, for it verified his new hypothesis of the direction of lightning. Franklin said that he had received a pane of glass and a letter from Kinnersley, telling of the latter's suspicions that the direction of the stroke of lightning was upwards. Further, he has written Kinnersley a short account of the experiment he made before he left home and referred him to William for the explanation according to the new hypothesis. In September, Franklin wrote to Peter Collinson that "Mr. Kinnersley returning from the Islands just as I left home, pursued the Experiments during my Absence, and informs me, that he always found the Clouds in the negative State." Kinnersley continued testing the electrical state of the clouds, inventing two new methods for determining whether they were positive or negative. He also performed a series of experiments on conductors, proving that metal is a better conductor than water; "Thus, though a small vial containing water will give a smart shock, one containing the same quantity of mercury will give one much stronger, the mercury being the better conductor; while one containing oil only, will scarce give any shock at all."[2]

Kinnersley installed his equipment in "one of the Chambers of the Academy," for his lectures, given several times a year for the next twenty-one years, (see Appendix II), were nearly always advertised as at "the Apparatus Room," familiarly known by the students as the Electricity Room.[3] Kinnersley's first advertisement after his return to Philadelphia was in the *Pennsylvania Gazette* for December 27, 1753. Even in Philadelphia, the birthplace of the discovery of the electrical nature of lightning, the religious

---

[2] Leonard W. Labaree, ed., and Whitfield J. Bell, Jr., assoc. ed., *The Papers of Benjamin Franklin* (New Haven and London, 1959—), V, 15, 71, 262, and 523.

[3] Edward Potts Cheyney, *History of the University of Pennsylvania* (Philadelphia, 1940), p. 75.

legality of the scientists' efforts to control natural phenomena was still in question:

> That the electric Element, produced by the Friction of Glass, &c. is the very same with Lightning, and subject to the same Laws; and that Houses, Ships, &c. may very easily be preserved from being ever damaged by Lightning. And as some are apt to doubt the Lawfulness of such Methods of Security, it will be further shewn that the endeavouring to guard against Lightning in the Manner proposed, cannot possibly be chargeable with Presumption, nor be inconsistent with any of the Principles either of natural or revealed Religion.[4]

Kinnersley followed the advances of electrical experimentation with an eye for what would appeal to the public. Georg Wilhelm Richmann, a Russian scientist born in the same year as Kinnersley (1711), was killed on August 6, 1753, while making an experiment "according to the Method practised by Mr. Franklin, of Philadelphia." Richmann, however, used an ungrounded test rod and was therefore struck by lightning. The note of the death of Richmann, that appeared in the *Pennsylvania Gazette,* March 5, 1754, explained:

> The new Doctrine of Lightning is, however, confirm'd by this unhappy Accident; and many Lives may hereafter be sav'd by the Practice it teaches. M. Richmann being about to make Experiments on the Matter of Lightning, had supported his Rod and Wires by Electrics *per se* [non-conductors], which cut off their Communication with the Earth; and himself standing too near where the Wire terminated, help'd with his Body to compleat that Communication. It is plain the Wire conducted the Lightning to him thro' the whole Length of the Gallery: And had his Apparatus been intended for the

---

[4] This direct statement of religious prejudice first appeared in Kinnersley's advertisements as No. 21 in his second lecture in his broadside dated St. John's, April 25, 1753. It is often included in his advertisements after 1753.

Security of his House, and the Wire (as in that Case it ought to be) continued without Interruption from the Roof to the Earth, it seems more than probable that the Lightning would have follow'd the Wire, and that neither the House nor any of the Family would have been hurt by that unfortunate Stroke.[5]

In his advertisement in the *Pennsylvania Gazette*, March 26, 1754, Kinnersley wrote that "the circumstances of the late unhappy Accident which befel Professor Richman, at Petersburgh, will also be explained, and be shewn to strongly confirm the . . . Doctrine" of the electrical nature of lightning.

In September, 1754, when Ezra Stiles (later President of Yale) visited Philadelphia, he recorded in his diary:

28. . . . Visited Academy. Mr. Alison Mastr Lat. School, £ 200; Mr. Eben Kinnersley, Mastr Eng. School, £ 150; Mr. Theoph. Grew, Math. Mastr, £ 120; Mr. Creamer, Mastr French & Italian & Dutch & Drawing, £ 100; Mr. Smith, Mastr of Phil., Math., & Moral. Orators,—Wm Kinnersley, Henry Merchant, Henry Benbridge, Thos Bond, Robt Jones, Jasper Yeates. Pastoral Speakers,—Andrew Hamilton & Wm Hamilton, Jno Okill. Morg. waited on Mr. Kennersly; he went with us to the Court House, where ye Supreme Court was sitting; heard Mr. Francis, Attorney General, and Mr. Moland plead a cause to the jury. . . . Walkd to Mr. Kennersly's. View'd the Academy apartments; heard Mr Duchee, a young gentleman, reading philosophy under Mr. Smith, pronounce Prologue of Cato, &c. & young Mr. Kennersly (about 11 aetat.), &c. Went up, & from top of the Academy viewed the city of Phila, . . . View'd the rods & wires which defend the Academy House from lightning. Viewed the bells, &c. in Mr Kennerslys house & electric rod. . . . Spent evening at our lodgings with Mr. Kennersly.

30. . . . waited on Mr. Kinnersley, who shewed his curious electrical apparatus, with sundry experiments, &c. . . . N.B. Shewed Mr Kinnersly Mr —— Poem on the Spring,

[5] Labaree, V, 220.

who was so well pleased with it that he requested me to leave it with him for the use of his young orators.[6]

On February 5, 1755, Stiles mentioned Kinnersley with honor in a latin oration at Yale celebrating Franklin. And later that year, Stiles sent his compliments to "Mr. Kennersly of whose Humanity I retain a grateful Remembrance."[7]

At the creation of the Philadelphia College in 1755, Kinnersley was unanimously chosen by the Trustees as Professor of the English Tongue and of Oratory.[8] Although Anglo-Saxon was offered in colleges in England, modern English wasn't taught until the last part of the nineteenth century. Kinnersley was probably the first person to have the title Professor of English. Unfortunately, with Franklin away, Kinnersley was not able to make the English curriculum a significant force in the college, and his duties there were probably largely restricted to teaching oratory and electricity.

In 1756, the great American grammarian Lindley Murray studied under Kinnersley. Murray later wrote:

At an early period, about my sixth or seventh year,[9] I was sent to the city of Philadelphia, that I might have the advantage of a better school that the country afforded. I well remember being some time at the academy of Philadelphia; the English Department of which was then conducted by the truly respectable Ebenezer Kinnersley. He exercised great care over his pupils, and from what I recollect of this instructor of youth,

---

[6] Edward G. Porter, ed., "Diary of Ezra Stiles," *Proceedings of the Massachusetts Historical Society,* 2d ser., VII (1891, 1892), 340–41, and 343.

[7] Labaree, V, 496 and 515.

[8] July 11, 1755. Minutes, I, 55.

[9] Lindley Murray was born in 1745. Thomas Harrison Montgomery, *A History of the University of Pennsylvania from its foundation to A.D. 1770* (Philadelphia, 1900), p. 546, records that Murray entered the Academy in 1756. Therefore, he was at least ten when he studied under Kinnersley.

and what I have read of him, I have reason to regret, that my continuance in that seminary was of short duration. I remember to have read there with pleasure, even at that age, some passages in the "Travels of Cyrus;" and to have been agreeably exercised in the business of parsing sentences.[10]

According to Franklin's plan, Andrew M. Ramsay's *The Travels of Cyrus* (one of the books included in the program at the suggestion of Samuel Johnson of New York) would have been taught in the sixth or highest class in the English Academy; parsing sentences, however, was a primary task in the second class.[11]

The best record of Kinnersley's curriculum and manner of teaching in the English School is by a former student, Alexander Graydon. Kinnersley followed the texts and methods suggested by Franklin in "Idea of the English School" (1751).[12] Franklin proposed that the boys begin by learning grammar and spelling, and that they learn oratory by imitating the master, who has "read the Piece with the proper Modulations of Voice, due Emphasis, and suitable Action." Graydon recorded in his *Memoirs*:

> Being now [1760], probably, about eight years of age, it was deemed expedient to enter me at the academy, then, as it now continues to be, under the name of a university, the principal seminary in Pennsylvania; and I was accordingly introduced by my father, to Mr. Kinnersley, the teacher of English and professor of oratory. He was an Anabaptist clergyman, a large, venerable looking man, of no great general erudition, though a considerable proficient in electricity; . . .
> The task, of the younger boys, at least, consisted in learning to read and to write their mother tongue grammatically; and one day in the week (I think Friday) was set apart for the

---

[10] Elizabeth Frank, *Memoirs of the Life and Writings of Lindley Murray* (New York, 1827), p. 8.
[11] Labaree, IV, 107 and 103.
[12] *Ibid.,* 101–08.

recitation of select passages in poetry and prose. For this purpose, each scholar, in his turn, ascended the stage, and said his speech, as the phrase was. This speech was carefully taught him by his master, both with respect to its pronunciation, and the action deemed suitable to its several parts. . . . More profit attended my reading. After Aesop's fables, and an abridgment of the Roman history, Telemachus was put into our hands; and if it be admitted that the human heart may be bettered by instruction, mine, I may aver, was benefitted by this work of the virtuous Fenelon. While the mild wisdom of Mentor called forth my veneration, the noble ardor of the youthful hero excited my sympathy and emulation. I took part, like a second friend, in the vicissitudes of his fortune, I participated in his toils, I warmed with his exploits, I wept where he wept, and exulted where he triumphed.[13]

In Franklin's "Idea of the English School," reading should begin with short pieces, such as "Croxhall's Fables." When the students were more advanced, "They may begin with Rollin's *Antient and Roman Histories,* and proceed at proper Hours as they go thro' the subsequent Classes, with the best Histories of our own Nation and Colonies." And Franklin wrote, "let such Lessons for Reading be chosen, as contain some useful Instruction; whereby the Understandings or Morals of the Youth, may at the same Time be improved."[14] Graydon testifies that *Telemachus,* which was to be taught in the sixth and highest class, did this for him.

William Smith, Provost of the College, at first followed Franklin's scheme of education, even incorporating Franklin's views into his own plan for a college. In Philadelphia, February 24, 1757, Smith wrote of the College and Academy, "One very considerable part in the plan of this

---

[13] Alexander Graydon, *Memoirs of a Life* . . . (Harrisburgh, 1811), pp. 16–17.
[14] Labaree, IV, 105, 104, and 103.

institution, is the *English school*, where the English language is taught grammatically, and where the youth are instructed in just *pronunciation* and *oratory.*" His reasons for the study of English in America are particularly interesting:

This branch of education, which is too much neglected in other institutions of the like kind, is found peculiarly necessary in the circumstances of this province, where the true pronunciation of the *English* language might soon be lost, without proper care to preserve it in the rising generation; as we are a mixture of people from almost all parts of the world, speaking a variety of languages and dialects.

Next, Smith gives a proud account of the students' oratorical training, which was responsible, according to him, for the performance of the *Masque of Alfred,* "The first native dramatic effort, containing original material and known to have been produced on the stage, that has come down to us."[15]

For the attaining of such a correct pronunciation, the youth are frequently exercised in delivering speeches from the parliamentary debates, or in acting scenes from our best tragedies, which they have, from time to time, performed before large audiences, with much success and great applause. At the same time that the lower schools are thus employed, the youth in the philosophy schools often deliver speeches of their own composition; so that no institution in the world can boast a better education in oratory than is to be found here.

Smith says that the students decided to give "a whole dramatic piece, as an oratorical exercise," and chose "Mr. Mallet's masque of Alfred."[16]

At the first commencement (May 17, 1757) of the Phila-

---

[15] Arthur Hobson Quinn, *A History of the American Drama From the Beginning to the Civil War* (New York, 1943), p. 18.
[16] William Smith, [Account of the College of Philadelphia], *Gentleman's Magazine*, XXVII (April, 1757), 177–79.

delphia College, Academy and Charitable School, Ebenezer Kinnersley was awarded the honorary degree of Master of Arts. Kinnersley continued his researches. Franklin's London account book reveals that Franklin purchased materials for him: September 20, 1757, "George Adam's bill for A. Taylor and Eb'r Kinnersley"; and December 5, 1757, "Mr. Kinnersley Dr. for globe."[17]

The *American Magazine* for January, 1758, contained an article by David Colden, the son of Cadwalader Colden, "New Experiments in Electricity." Kinnersley differed with Colden's conclusions and refuted them in "Further Experiments in Electricity."[18] David Colden prepared three drafts of his reply to Kinnersley's article, and his reply "To Mr. E. K. of Philadelphia" appeared in the *New American Magazine* in April, 1759.[19] Kinnersley did not seem to feel it worthwhile to reply to Colden—but this interchange demonstrates that Kinnersley was, after Franklin, the foremost electrical experimenter and theorist active in America. Further evidence of Kinnersley's pre-eminence is found in William Johnson's correspondence with David Colden. William Johnson was the second most famous lecturer on electricity in colonial America. His lectures were based on Kinnersley's. Johnson toured America from 1763 to his death, at forty-two years of age, on December 29, 1768.[20] In Johnson's

[17] George Simpson Eddy, ed., "Account Book . . . Kept by him during his First Mission to England as Provincial Agent, 1752–1756," *Pennsylvania Magazine of History and Biography*, LV (1931), 103 and 106.

[18] *The American Magazine and Monthly Chronicle for the British Colonies*, I (1758), 165–66, and 627–30.

[19] *The Letters and Papers of Cadwalader Colden* (New York Historical Society, *Collections*, for 1917–1923, 1934, 1935), VII (1923), 362. *New American Magazine*, I (1759), 422–25.

[20] Johnson, an Irish Friend, settled in Philadelphia in 1754. He probably learned electricity from Kinnersley. In addition to the evidence in his letter to Colden, there is the curious fact that he

letter to David Colden dated December 7, 1763, he refers to his "letter to the reverend Mr. E. Kinnersley on electrical repulsion."[21] Obviously, electricians in America turned to Kinnersley for expert opinion.

By 1758, Kinnersley was discouraged with his position at the College and Academy. Perhaps he had hoped that the Professor of English and Oratory would have a number of intellectually challenging duties at the recently organized College. By this time, however, he knew that the training at the College was primarily classical and that his services there were of use mainly as a Professor of Oratory. It may be that Kinnersley was dissatisfied with his position for some other reason, but the reply Franklin gave him, in a letter dated July 28, 1759, suggests that Franklin thought Kinnersley was dissatisfied with the program or with the administration:

> I received your favour of Sept. 9 [1758?] and should have answer'd it sooner, but delay'd in Expectation of procuring for you some Book that describes and explains the Uses of the Instruments you are at a loss about. . . . You do not mention the Reason of your being tired of your Situation in the

seems not to have lectured in Philadelphia, the largest city at this time in the colonies and, of course, Kinnersley's home. Johnson's advertisements include: *New York Gazette,* October 13 and 31, 1763, January 13, 1766 ; *New York Mercury,* October 24 and 31, 1763 ; *Newport Mercury,* February 6, 13, and 20, 1764 ; *Providence Gazette,* March 3, 1764 ; *Boston Gazette,* August 12, 1765 ; *Virginia Gazette* (Purdie & Dixon), October 10, 1766 ; and the *South Carolina Gazette,* April 13, May 4 and 18, 1765, February 9, 16, and 24, June 1, and December 14, 1767. Two editions of his syllabus are extant, *A Course of Experiments in Electricity* (New York, 1764, and New York, 1765). His obituary appeared in the *South Carolina Gazette* for January 5, 1769, and was reprinted in part in the *Boston Post-Boy* for February 13, 1769. Dr. Whitfield J. Bell, Jr., who is preparing a biographical dictionary of early members of the American Philosophical Society, kindly allowed me to use his notes on Johnson, an APS member.

[21] *Colden Papers,* VI (for 1922), 255.

Academy. And if you had, it would perhaps be out of my
Power at this Distance to remedy any Inconveniences you
suffer or even if I was present. For before I left Philadelphia,
everything to be done in the Academy was privately precon-
certed in a Cabal without my Knowledge or Participation and
accordingly carried into Execution. The Schemes of Public
Parties made it seem requisite to lessen my Influence where-
ever it could be lessened. . . .

I once thought of advising you to make Trial of your
Lectures here, and perhaps in the more early Times of Electricity it might have answered; but now I much doubt it, so
great is the general Negligence of every thing in the Way of
Science that has not Novelty to recommend it. Courses of
Experimental Philosophy, formerly so much in Vogue, are
now disregarded; so that Mr. Demainbray, who is reputed an
excellent Lecturer, and has an Apparatus that cost nearly
£ 2000, the finest perhaps in the World, can hardly make up an
audience in this great City to attend one Course in a Winter.

Franklin took the role of his old friend Peter Collinson in
transmitting news of the latest developments in the sciences
to the colonies:

But the greatest Discovery in this Way is the Virtue of the
Tourmalin Stone, brought from Ceylon in the Indies which
being heated in boiling Water, becomes strongly electrical, one
side positive, the other negative, without the least Rubbing.
They are very rare but I have two of them & long to show
you the Experiments.

Billy joins with me in Compliments to you & to good Mrs.
Kinnersley & your promising Children. I am with much
Esteem and Affection Dear Sir,

                              Your most obedient Servant
                              B. Franklin[22]

---

[22] Horatio Gates Jones, "Letter of Benjamin Franklin to Professor
Kinnersley," *Pennsylvania Magazine of History and Biography*,
XIII (1889), 247–48.

Kinnersley was ill in August, 1759, but better by September.[23] In October of 1760, Kinnersley and Dr. John Redman were supposed to supervise "the repairing the Academy Fences and Pavement." But "they acquainted the Trustees that tho they had taken all the pains in their power, that there was such a demand for Bricks and Workmen for the Buildings now going on in the City, and that tho they were promised them time after time, yet they were always disappointed."[24]

On March 12, 1761, Kinnersley wrote his most important letter on electricity. He questioned a cardinal point in the Franklinian system—the doctrine of repulsion. Franklin gave Kinnersley's argument a detailed examination, admitted that he wasn't entirely satisfied with his own explanation, and concluded, "We should not, indeed, multiply causes in philosophy without necessity; and the greater simplicity of your hypothesis would recommend it to me, if I could see that all appearances would be solved by it. But I find, or think I find, the two causes more convenient than one of them alone."[25] Kinnersley told Franklin of his experiment testing whether the amount of electricity in the air is the same "at the height of two or three hundred yards, as near the surface of the earth." He concluded that the electricity at the times tested was denser above than below. Characteristically, Kinnersley thought of his possible audience, and rigged up "a light horse, with his rider"; "each courser urged on by an electrised point instead of a pair of spurs, I was entertained with an electrical horse-race."

In this letter Kinnersley disclosed his most famous invention: "I have contrived an electrical air thermometer, and

---

[23] Minutes, I, 106.
[24] Ibid., 124.
[25] I. Bernard Cohen, *Benjamin Franklin's Experiments* (Cambridge, Massachusetts, 1941), pp. 366–67.

made several experiments with it, that have afforded me much satisfaction and pleasure." Kinnersley then tells Franklin that "lightning does not melt by a cold fusion" as they had formerly supposed, but that "electric fire . . . will, by its violent motion, and the resistance it meets with, produce heat in other bodies when passing through them." Kinnersley says that his electric air thermometer "fully determines that controversial point, Whether there be any heat in the electric fire?" Kinnersley also describes the effect of lightning on a house which had been struck by it, but protected by a lightning rod. The point of the rod, confirming Kinnersley's theory that electricity produces heat, was melted. Kinnersley sent a "draught" and a description of his thermometer with the letter, as well as "the best representation I can give" of the melted point of the lightning rod. Unfortunately, Kinnersley's drawings are no longer extant but engravings made for the published letter are (see illustration). This letter was read before the Royal Society on November 18, 1762, March 24, and April 14, 1763. It was published in the *Philosophical Transactions* and in the fourth English edition of Franklin's *Experiments and Observations* (1769) and consequently in subsequent editions.[26]

On July 14, 1761, the Trustees of the Philadelphia Academy visited the "English and Mathematical Schools, Dr. Alison and Mr. Alison the Latin Usher renewed their application for an Augmentation of their Saleries.—And Mr. Kinnersley likewise requested that the Trustees would be pleased to make him a larger Allowance, his present one not being sufficient to support his family." On the twelfth of January, 1762, "The Trustees desired Mr. Kinnersley to

[26] *Ibid.,* pp. 348–58. Ebenezer Kinnersley, "New Experiments in Electricity," *Philosophical Transactions of the Royal Society of London,* LIII (1763), 84–97.

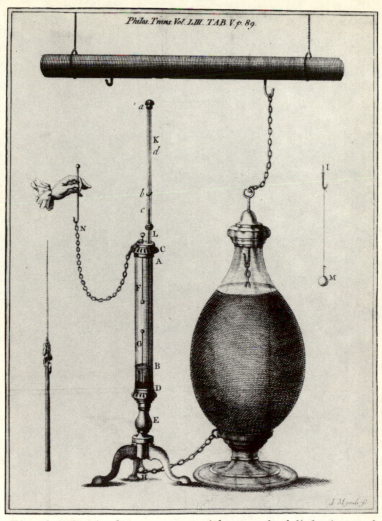

The electric air thermometer, with a melted lightning rod

be present, and after examining the several matters set forth by him in his Petition they agreed that he should have £30 additional Salary for the succeeding Year." And as there were over fifty boys in the English school, Mr. Davis was appointed to assist him at £25 per annum.[27]

Without Franklin's influence, the English school was allowed by the Trustees to dwindle in importance. On February 8, 1763, Kinnersley reported that his time was taken up with teaching little boys the elements of the English language. On April 12, 1763, a committee was appointed to confer on the state of the English school. On June 13, the Trustees recorded:

> Some of the parents of the Children in the Academy had complained that their Children were not taught to speak and read in public, and having requested that this useful part of Education might be more attended to. Mr. Kinnersley was called in and desired to give an account of what was done in this Branch of his duty; and he declared that this was well taught not only in the English School which was more immediately under his care, but in the Philosophy Classes regularly every Monday afternoon, and as often at other times as his Business would permit. And it not appearing to the Trustees that any more could at present be done without partiality and great inconvenience and that this was all that was proposed to be done, they did not incline to make any alteration, or to lay any Burthen upon Mr. Kinnersley.[28]

Franklin, in his *Observations Relative to the Intentions of the Original Founders of the Academy in Philadelphia,* noted that the Latin Master was supposed to help the English Master, and that the reverse wasn't part of the original plan.[29] The English school was of less importance to Provost

---

[27] Minutes, I, 142 and 163–64.
[28] *Ibid.,* 192 and 200.
[29] Thomas Woody, *Educational Views of Benjamin Franklin* (New York and London, 1931), pp. 210–11.

Smith and the Trustees than the Latin school. Not only did the Master of the Latin school receive a greater salary, but the ushers of the English school were often promoted to the Latin school after they had satisfactorily demonstrated their ability in the English school [30]

In 1764, the syllabus for Kinnersley's lectures, by this time an institution in Philadelphia, was printed. Reverend Henry Melchior Muhlenberg recorded that on December 27, 1764, "I was invited to attend a cursus physico-experimentalis at the local Academy, where Professor Ebenezer Kinnersley exhibited some excellent experiments in electricity." And on Friday, the 28th, he attended the second lecture.[31]

Kinnersley was appointed steward of the "New Building" (which combined classrooms and dormitory) at a meeting of the trustees on September 11, 1764. The *Pennsylvania Gazette* for January 31, 1765, announced the opening of the New Building, "accommodating about 60 students." "The Reverend Mr. Ebenezer Kinnersley, one of the Professors, a Gentleman of regular and exemplary Life, hath undertaken the particular Management and Stewardship of same." In answer to Kinnersley's question of his jurisdiction over the students living in the dormitory, the Trustees, on November 19, 1765, said that they:

> think it necessary in general to declare, that as they cannot, without further Trial, frame Rules that may provide against all possible cases, it was their intention to give Mr. Kinnersley all the Powers necessary for preserving good order among the Youth in the said Buildings; and that he may and ought in ordinary Cases to exercise such Discretionary Authority

---

[30] Montgomery, p. 472.

[31] Theodore G. Tappert and John W. Doberstein, translators, *The Journals of Henry Melchior Muhlenberg* (Philadelphia, 1942–1958), II, 159.

as a Father would in the government of his own Family; and in difficult cases to take the Advice and Assistance of the Faculty of Masters or to consult the Trustees when the case may require it.[32]

In 1767, Kinnersley received high praise in Joseph Priestley's monumental *History and Present State of Electricity*: "Some of his [Kinnersley] observations . . . are very curious; and some later accounts, which he himself has transmitted to England, seem to promise, that, if he continue his electrical inquiries, his name, after that of his friend [Franklin], will be second to few in the history of electricity."[33] On March 20, 1767, Kinnersley was elected a member of the American Society for Promoting Useful Knowledge; and on January 26, 1768, he was chosen a member of the American Philosophical Society. Kinnersley's scientific experiments were not limited to electricity: David Rittenhouse, speculating on the compressibility of water, wrote to Thomas Barton on March 27, 1767, that he "had not then met with any person who had seen Mr. Kinnersley's experiment on that theory; but that he understood it was made with the air-pump, and conjectured it to have been similar to the one made by a member of the Royal Society, related in *Martin's Magazine*."[34]

Kinnersley's duties as steward of the New Building are revealed by the report on December 15, 1767, of Dr. William Shippen and John Inglis:

They have visited the Lodgers and Apartments in the new Buildings, and have read the original Regulations made for their Management and Government, from which it appears,

[32] Minutes, I, 262; Montgomery, p. 447.
[33] Joseph Priestley, *History and Present State of Electricity* (London, 1767), pp. 187-88.
[34] William Barton, *Memoirs of David Rittenhouse* (Philadelphia, 1813), pp. 155–56.

that the care of the Boys with respect to their Linnen, Comb-
ing their Heads and other matters, in which the younger part
of them could not be trusted to themselves, had always been
considered as part of the Steward's Duty, for the Allowance
made to Him. And that Mr. Kinnersley had assured them that
he had always taken care to see that their Chambers were
kept clean, and that Mrs. Kinnersley sends for the smaller
Boys twice every Week to have their Heads combed, and that
every Monday they are ordered to bring their dirty Linnen to
her, with a List of them, to be given out to be washed, and that
she receives them back according to the list. They report
further that on visiting the Rooms, they found them clean,
and the Provisions good that were intended for that Day's
Dinner. And as Mr. Kinnersley engages to continue his
utmost care in these matters, they think there can be no just
ground for Complaint.[35]

In 1769, the Trustees proposed to discontinue the English
school, but an examination of their charter and constitution
revealed that they were unable to do so. Their desire to
discard the English school was probably due partially to
the financial burden of maintaining the school, and partially
to the traditional belief that English was not a proper subject
for advanced study. In addition, Kinnersley had told them
that he intended to resign to go to the West Indies for his
health. But his health continued to hold up, so he stayed on
at the Academy. On October 17, 1769, he announced his
decision to stay at the Academy until "next spring on such
Terms as the Trustees might judge reasonable." He was paid
£200 a year and his home was rent-free.[36]

Sometime around 1770, the Reverend Morgan Edwards,
the minister of Philadelphia's Baptist Church, placed his

---

[35] Montgomery, p. 448.
[36] Minutes, II, 9, 12, 14, and 19.

son Joshua in the Academy to study under Kinnersley. Joshua, in a brief autobiography, later wrote:

Owing to either his father's settled opinion that education can not be commenced too soon, nor too actively carried forward; or to the influence of a very cordial friendship that subsisted between that careful guardian and a Rev. Mr. Kinnersley, who then occupied, with great reputation, the Professor's Chair of the Academical department of the Philadelphia College,—the narrator was, at the dawning of his seventh year, placed in that classical seminary, the rules of which were absolute; its discipline rigid, its exercises measured out by a liberal scale and exactness of performance insisted upon. . . . During Summer two extra hours of attendance, from six to eight in the morning, and even the holydays had their prescribed tasks.[37]

On October 13, 1770, Kinnersley wrote Franklin an account of some experiments he had made on the conductivity of various kinds of charcoal. This was read before the Royal Society on December 10, 1772, and published in the *Philosophical Transactions*.[38]

Kinnersley resigned his "Office and Professorship" in the Philadelphia College, Academy and Charitable School effective October 17, 1772, because "the present state of his health" required that he spend the approaching winter in a warmer climate. Kinnersley said that he hoped the Trustees would give him a certificate of his good behaviour for the nineteen years that he had spent in their service, and the Trustees also granted his request to "allow Mrs. Kinnersley to occupy the House in which he now lives, till next Spring."[39]

---

[37] Quoted from William Williams Keen. *The Bi-centennial Celebration of the Founding of the First Baptist Church of the City of Philadelphia* (Philadelphia, 1899), p. 48, n. 2.

[38] Ebenezer Kinnersley, "On some electrical experiments made with charcoal," *Philosophical Transactions* LXIII, pt. 1 (1773), 38–39.

[39] Minutes, II, 55.

The last and perhaps most surprising tribute to the effectiveness of Kinnersley's lectures appeared in the *Pennsylvania Gazette,* November 11, 1772:

> On Saturday last Kayashuta, the great Seneca Chief, returned to this city from Johnson-hall, where he has been on a visit to Sir William Johnson, of the greatest Importance to the Colonies. The Entertainment he received, when last here, at seeing a few Electrical Experiments, has so much engaged his attention and admiration, that we are informed, his first Enquiry at his Return was, whether he could have another Opportunity of seeing Thunder and Lightning produced by human art? And we hear, he is determined to attend Mr. Kinnersley's Lectures at the College, on Thursday and Friday Evenings next.
>
> We are informed that Mr. Kinnersley intends to continue his Lectures here no longer than next Week, and the Week after.[40]

Kinnersley left for Barbados in the Brig *Rachel* with Captain L. Simmons during the week preceding December 16, 1772.[41]

On February 2, 1773, the Trustees recorded that "the College suffers greatly since Mr. Kinnersley left it for want of a person to teach public speaking; so that the present classes have not those opportunities of learning to declaim and speak, which have been of so much use to their predecessors, and have contributed greatly to raise the Credit of the Institution."[42] In the *Pennsylvania Gazette,* October 13, 1773, William Smith, Provost of the College, advertised for "A Person capable of Teaching the English Language Grammatically, and who understands Algebra, Euclid's Elements and the practical Branches of the Mathematics."

---

[40] Reprinted in Rind's, and Purdie and Dixon's *Virginia Gazette,* December 3, 1772.

[41] *Pennsylvania Gazette,* December 16, 1772.

[42] Minutes, II, 60.

On March 13, 1773, Kinnersley wrote to his wife from
Bridge-Town:

My dearest love,

I am here in Barbados yet but have done but little good for
myself or any body else.[43] The weather has been very damp
most of the time I have been here, and people complain much
of the Scarcity of money. I have detained so long, that I have
dropt all thoughts of going to Jamaica. If Captain Symmons
comes again while I stay, I like him and his vessal so well, that
I shall be glad of the opportunity to return home with him.
Caesar was taken very ill last week with a pain in his bowels,
which at last settled in his side, bleeding and some doses of
physick has made him pretty well again. My lameness con-
tinues much the same, I know no more of Mrs. Bishop's
affairs than when I wrote last. I wrote to Mr. Walker the day
before yesterday, acquainting him that I intend to leave the
island in a few weeks, and should be glad to have [. . .] settled
before [. . .] no Answer. . . . My best wishes and most
fervent prayers will always attend you, my dearest love, as
long as I remain on this side the grave. As I undertook this
voyage solely with a view of promoting our mutual Advantage,
in hopes of having something to support us comfortably in
the decline of life, if providence should think best to disappoint
the pleasing expectation, I hope to learn submission to the
Sovereign Disposer of all things, and to find in your
sympathising breast when I return, a kind and hearty welcome
to comfort you

affectionate husband[44]

Kinnersley returned to Philadelphia in June, 1773, to find
that his daughter, Esther (Kinnersley) Shewell, had died.[45]

---

[43] Kinnersley evidently gave lectures in Barbados.
[44] Photostats of this letter are in the American Baptist Historical
Society and the Historical Society of Pennsylvania. Printed with the
permission of the Historical Society of Pennsylvania.
[45] Francis Alison to his son Dr. Benjamin Alison, June 10, 1773.
Historical Society of Pennsylvania.

On July 30, 1773, at a meeting of the American Philosophical Society, Kinnersley, Isaac Bartram, David Rittenhouse,
Levi Hollingsworth, and Owen Biddle were instructed to
"agree with the Owner of the Torpedo [an electric eel], on
terms to make a Set of Experiments, with a view to determine
the nature of the Shocks which it communicates."[46] The
electric eel was currently the subject of much experimentation. In Charleston, Dr. Alexander Garden wrote a natural-
ist's account of the eel which appeared in the *Philosophical
Transactions* of the Royal Society in 1775.[47] The experiments
made by Kinnersley and others on August 17 and 18, 1773,
were published by Benjamin Smith Barton in the *Philadelphia Medical and Physical Journal* in 1805.[48] Kinnersley
led the experiments, performed "For the purpose of ascer-
taining the nature of the faculty by which this fish is enabled,
on being touched, to impart a shock, very similar in sensation
to that produced by the electric fluid." Contemporary newspaper accounts of the experiments reported:

> We hear from Philadelphia, that there is now in that City,
> a live Fish supposed to be a *Torpedo,* which on being touched,
> gives a very strong electrical Shock, to any number of Persons
> whose Hands are in Contact with each other; several Persons
> affected with various Disorders, have found Relief from it,
> when the common Mode of electerizing has proved ineffectual.
> It has been observed, that after receiving a Shock from the
> Fish, it takes some Time to recover the like Quantity of
> electrical Fluid; and that if touched sooner, the Shocks are

---

[46] American Philosophical Society, *Proceedings,* XXII (1885), 66.
[47] Alexander Garden, "Account of the Gymnotus electricus,"
Philosophical Transactions, LXV (1775), 102–10.
[48] David Rittenhouse, "Experiments on the Gymnotus Electricus,
or Electric Eel, made at Philadelphia, about the year 1770, by the
late Mr. Rittenhouse, Mr. E. Kinnersley, and some other gentlemen,"
Philadelphia Medical and Physical Journal, I, pt. 2 (1805), 96–100,
and 159–61.

weak or strong in proportion to the Time since the preceeding Shock.[49]

On December 29, 1773, Kinnersley, again incorporating the latest discoveries, fads, and techniques in electricity, ran his advertisement in its final form in the *Pennsylvania Gazette*:

For the Entertainment of the Curious,

Mr. Kinnersley having lately made some considerable addition to his Electrical Apparatus, particularly, having added an elegant case of seventy bottles, each lined and coated with tinfoil, he proposes to exhibit a course of ELECTRICAL EXPERIMENTS, at the College in this city, on Monday and Tuesday next week; and again on the following Wednesday and Friday to begin at six o'clock in the evening. In this course, consisting of only two lectures, above forty curious and interesting experiments will be exhibited, tending to shew the nature and properties of lightning, and, which is of the greatest importance, how to avoid the danger of it; how to secure houses, ships, &c. from receiving any damage by lightning.

The following particulars will, it is presumed, be thought no inconsiderable part of this Electrical Experiment, *viz.* Flashes of real lightning visible under water. Iron heated red hot, and even melted by lightning, whilst under, and in contact with, common cold water. Experiments on that wonderful electric stone from the East-Indies, called the Tourmalin, which will become electrified by being dipt in boiling water; one side electrified positively, the other negatively. A curious representation of the astonishing electric eel, lately seen in this city, on touching of which, while in the water, an electric shock may be as sensibly felt, as from a live one. A representa-

---

[49] *Boston Evening Post*, August 30, 1773. This was reprinted from a New York newspaper of August 23, 1773. It was also printed in the *Massachusetts Gazette* and the *Massachusetts Spy*, August 26, 1773.

tion of part of the starry heavens, exhibiting a variety of beautiful electric stars.

As the knowledge of Nature tends to enlarge the human mind, and give us more noble and exalted ideas of the Author of Nature, and, if well pursued, seldom fails producing something useful to man; it is hoped that an entertainment of such a tendency will meet with suitable encouragement. Those Gentlemen and Ladies who purpose to attend these lectures, are requested to be furnished with tickets, that no money may be taken at the door. Tickets may be had at the bar of the London Coffee-house; and at Mr. Kinnersley's house, near the College, at Half a Dollar for each lecture.

N.B. Electrical Experiments cannot be well exhibited in damp or wet weather; therefore if either of the evenings above appointed should not prove dry enough, the exhibition must be deferred till some dry evening after. The first lecture of each course to be on Monday and Wednesday evenings; second lecture on Tuesday and Friday evenings.

His advertisements continued through January and February of 1774, and on March 2, 1774, Kinnersley's last advertisement for his lectures on electricity appeared in the *Pennsylvania Gazette.*

In the spring of 1774 the revolutionary spirit was mounting. After the Philadelphians learned of Alexander Wedderburn's abusive treatment of Franklin before the Privy Council, they drove effigies of Wedderburn and Thomas Hutchinson (the royal governor of Massachusetts) around the city in a cart, then hung them, and then—by electricity—burned them "in the Evening amidst a vast Concourse of People, who testified their Resentment against the Originals with the loudest Acclamations."[50] Although there was another lecturer in electricity present in Philadelphia at least through

---

[50] *Pennsylvania Gazette,* May 4, 1774; cf. *Pennsylvania Packet,* May 9.

February,[51] it is generally agreed that Ebenezer Kinnersley burned Wedderburn and Hutchinson by electricity.[52]

Kinnersley probably continued to live at the College, acting as steward, until late in 1774 or some time in 1775. His advertisement of February 9, 1774, announced, "Next April Mr. Kinnersley expects to have room in his house to accommodate two or three more young Boarders for the College." The Provincial Tax for 1774 reveals that he was then living in Philadelphia and that he paid £4 for a servant.[53] However, in 1775 his health began to decline. It was probably in this year that he moved back to Moreland Township in Philadelphia County, back to the area of his childhood, near the Pennepack Baptist Church at Lower Merion. Here, his wife's relations, the Duffields, were to provide companionship for Franklin's family while the British occupied Philadelphia in 1777–1778. Kinnersley drew up his will on October 10, 1775. In the middle of March, 1778, while the British forces occupied Philadelphia, the Reverend Ebenezer Kinnersley, A.M., died at the age of sixty-seven. He was buried in the Pennepack graveyard.[54] In the turmoil of the times, no obituary of Kinnersley was published.

On December 15, 1778, at a meeting of the Trustees of the Philadelphia College:

> Dr. Smith informed the Board that some years ago Mr. Kinnersley had made an offer to the College of his Electrical Apparatus, and the several Fixtures belonging to it upon a valuation to be made by some proper Judges, that the Trustees

---

[51] Arthur John O'Neile's advertisements appeared in the *Pennsylvania Packet* for February 14 and 28, 1774.

[52] Carl and Jessica Bridenbaugh, *Rebels and Gentlemen* (New York, 1942), p. 332.

[53] *Pennsylvania Archives,* 3d ser., XIV, 270.

[54] "Tombstone Inscriptions From the Penepeck Graveyard," *Notes and Queries, Historical, Biographical and Genealogical,* 1899 (Harrisburg, 1900), p. 152. All the standard accounts list the date of his death as July 4, 1778, but no authority is given. Sir Charles

were then disposed to accept of the Proposal but that thro' the Disturbance of the Times the Business had not been compleated—That Mr. Kinnersley being since deceased, the apparatus by order of his Executors had been valued at about five hundred Pounds, was now in compleat Order and perhaps equal to any apparatus of the Kind in the World, and therefore proper to be kept, as it stands for the use of the College.

The Trustees who are present are of opinion that the said apparatus should be taken at the Valuation set upon it for the use of the College, and that it be inserted in the Notices to be given of next meeting, that money is proposed to be laid out, in order to have a full authority for this purchase.

And on December 23, 1778, the Trustees voted to "pay Mrs. Kinnersley, on Account of the College for the Electrical Apparatus, as the same has been valued by Mr. Rittenhouse and Mr. Bringhurst, and that the Inventory thereof be procured and inserted in the minutes."[55] The Day Book reveals that on December 31, 1778, £550 was paid to Edward Duffield, one of Kinnersley's executors, for the electrical apparatus. However, no inventory was inserted in the minutes, and no trace of Kinnersley's apparatus can now be found at the University of Pennsylvania.

An opponent of the enthusiastic tendencies of the Great Religious Awakening, colonial America's greatest scientific popularizer and greatest lecturer, a scientist in the pioneer field of electricity, and a teacher of the most enlightened English program of the eighteenth century in the colonies and perhaps in the world, Ebenezer Kinnersley held a minor position of considerable importance in the study of American culture.

Blagden wrote to Sir Joseph Banks from Philadelphia on March 26, 1778, that Kinnersley, "an ingenious local man," had just died. Warren R. Dawson, ed., *The Banks Letters, A Calendar . . .* (London, 1958), p. 52.

[55] Minutes, II, 117–18.

Appendix I

The Right of Private Judgment

The Pennsylvania Gazette, January 19, 1747/8

The grand Basis of the Reformation, and Support of the *Protestant* Causes, is the *Right of private Judgment*. But I renounce all Methods of Imposition, Violence and Persecution, not *merely* because they are *Popish,* but because they are Unnatural, Inhuman and Antichristian; and I plead for the Right of private Judgment, not *merely* as 'tis a *Protestant* Claim, but as 'tis one of those *sacred* and *original* Rights of human Nature, which the Gospel has revived and re-established.

Man is, by his *original Constitution,* a moral and accountable Being. And from hence it follows, that the Rights of Conscience are sacred and *equal* in all; that as every one is accountable for *himself,* he shall be allowed to reason, judge and determine, for himself; and as his Character for Virtue or Vice, Religion or Irreligion, depends entirely on *his own* Judgment, and *his* Choice, and not at all on that of others, both his Sentiments and Conduct, in Matters that *purely* relate to Conscience, and do not *directly* affect the Security and Welfare of Societies, should be *free* and *uncontroul'd.* A careful Examination, and free Choice for our Religion, appears to be the chief End for which we were endued with Reason: For if the great Creator design'd that the Bulk of Mankind should submit implicitly to a certain Sett of establish'd

113

Opinions; Reason, except only in the Compilers and Conductors of the publick Faith, must be in a great Measure *impertinent* and *useless*. Nay, it would be a very *absurd* and *unruly* Ingredient in our Composition; which, unless it were well disciplin'd, and kept under severe Command. would be apt to rebel against Authority, to question its Decisions, and believe nothing but what was intelligible in itself, and had good Evidence to support it. The Right of *private Judgment* is indeed an *unalienable* Right, which so directly results from our Make, and is so inseparably connected with it, that the one cannot be abrogated or invaded, without destroying or offering Violence to the other. A Man may alienate his Labour, his Estate, and several Branches of his Property, and give up his Right in them to others; but he can't transfer the *Rights of Conscience*, unless he could efface his moral and rational Faculties, and substitute another to be judged for him at the righteous Tribunal of God.

If all Christians were duly sensible of the Value of that inestimable Privilege which I am now pleading for; if they made a proper Use of it, and were honest and diligent in the Pursuit of Truth; if they proceeded in all their religious Inquiries with Candour and Impartiality, and were neither corrupted by irregular Passions, nor prevented by Prejudice, nor enslaved by Education, nor controuled and awed by the Restraints and Terrors of human Authority, whether Civil or Ecclesiastical; such an *Openness* and *Ingenuity* of Mind, such a *cool, disinterested* and *free* Examination of the Grounds of Religion, and the Principles it contains, must be attended with eminent Advantages to themselves, to Christianity, and Mankind in general. If Freedom of Thought and rational Enquiry universally prevail'd, Men could not be so easily practis'd upon by every *insinuating crafty,* or *bold* Impostor; but if their Understandings are brib'd or terrified, and either of these Ways brought to a tame and servile Submission to *imposed* and *popular* Opinions, to receive implicitly whatever the Church has set her *Stamp* upon, or has been transmitted down by a *solemn* Tradition from their Forefathers; they must of Necessity be exposed to endless Delusions, to the most *stupid impious* and *hurtful* Superstition, and may easily be *cajol'd* or *frighten'd* out of their Senses, and the common Principles of Humanity.

Another great Use of allowing the People to judge for themselves, both of the Proofs of Christianity, and the Nature of its Doctrines, is this, that they will of Course be more firmly establish'd in the Belief of it; whereas an implicit Faith, or the believing what we don't understand, we know not why, must be soon *baffled* and *unhinged*, and naturally tends to *Scepticism* and *Infidelity*.

And now, if the Right of every Man to determine, by *his own Reason*, what Scheme of Religion is most worthy of God, and most acceptable to him, be not only attended with signal Advantages, but *natural*, and *absolutely unalienable;* it follows, that no Constitutions and Rules of civil Society can be just, that are inconsistent with this Right; nay farther, that no true divine Revelation can either wholly destroy, or *restrain* and *limit*, the Exercise of it. So that if Christianity had really abridg'd that Freedom of Enquiry about religious Principles, which cannot be denied to any Man without supposing that he is neither an *intelligent* nor an *accountable* Being, this would have been such a strong *intrinsick* Mark of Imposture, as the Plea of Miracles could hardly have *counterbalanc'd*.

But if the direct Reverse of this be the Truth, if the Gospel frankly recommends to Men the Use and Improvement of their *rational Faculties;* if it invites to, and encourages the *strictest* and most *critical* Inquiries, and submits its Pretensions to the *Test* of sober unprejudic'd Reason; if we find, in the sacred Records of our Religion, the first Christians commended for discovering a *Nobleness* and *Ingenuity* of Temper, because they search'd the Scriptures, and such *Apostolical* Exhortations as these frequently inculcated, to be *Men in Understanding, to prove all Things, try the Spirits, whether they are of God,* and *judge* for ourselves *what is right.* And if the great God himself has appealed to human Reason, which is so much disgrac'd and vilified, as to the Enquiry of his Proceedings, and the general Rules by which he governs the moral World: What must we think of the Men, who, pretending to be Ambassadors from Heaven, and *infallible Interpreters* of the Divine Will, would fain persuade Christians, in these latter Times, to renounce their Understandings, in order to be religious, and to be *blind* and *indolent,* that they may more clearly perceive the pure Light of the Gospel?

Appendix II

Kinnersley's Advertisements in the *Pennsylvania Gazette*

1751	Apr. 11			Mar. 26
	Apr. 18			Sep. 17
	May 2			Sep. 24
1752	Sep. 14			Oct. 15
	Sep. 21			Dec. 7
	Sep. 28			Dec. 24
	Oct. 19		1762	Apr. 8
1753	Dec. 27			Dec. 23
1754	Mar. 26			Dec. 30
	Apr. 4		1763	Mar. 31
	Apr. 11			Dec. 22
	Dec. 12			Dec. 29
	Dec. 26		1764	Apr. 19
1755	Mar. 18			Dec. 20
	Mar. 25			Dec. 27
	Dec. 25		1765	Apr. 18
1756	Apr. 8			Dec. 19
1757	Dec. 22		1766	Jan. 2
1758	Dec. 28			Dec. 25
1759	Dec. 27		1767	Jan. 8
1760	Jan. 31			Jan. 15
	Dec. 25			Dec. 17
1761	Jan. 8		1769	Dec. 28
	Mar. 12		1770	Sep. 20
	Mar. 19			Dec. 20

117

	Dec. 27		Nov. 11
1771	Jan. 3		Nov. 18
	Dec. 26	1773	Dec. 29
	Feb. 28	1774	Jan. 5
1772	Jan. 2		Jan. 12
	Jan. 9		Jan. 19
	Jan. 30		Feb. 9
	Feb. 6		Feb. 16
	Feb. 13		Feb. 23
	Oct. 28		Mar. 2
	Nov. 4		

Appendix III

Kinnersley's Will

Be it Remembered that I Ebenezer Kinnersley of the city of Philadelphia in the province of Pennsylvania late Professor of English and Oratory in the College and Academy of Philadelphia, being weak and infirm in Body but, blessed be God, of sound and well disposing Mind and Memory, and being mindful of the uncertainty of Life do make this my last Will and Testament in Manner and Form following: that is to say,—First, It is my Will that as soon as conveniently may be after my decease, all my just debts and funeral charges be paid. Item. I give and bequeath unto my son William Kinnersley the sum of One Hundred and Fifty Pounds, and all my wearing Apparel. Item, I give and bequeath unto my three Grand Children Sarah, Benjamin and Elizabeth Shewell the sum of fifty pounds to each, that is to say to each of the girls when she arrives to the Age of Eighteen years or marries, and to the boy when he arrives to the Age of Twenty-one years. Item. All the remainder of my estate, except such few thereof as is already out on interest and excepting my household furniture, I desire may be sold and the Money to be put out on interest on good securities, and the interest arising therefrom, together with that arising from money I have already at interest, I do give and bequeath the same unto my beloved wife Sarah during her natural life, and after her decease, one moiety of the Principal and Interest then due, I give and bequeath to my son William and the other moiety thereof to my said three Grand children, share and share alike. But if either of my said

Grand children should Die under age or unmarried as aforesaid, I order that his or her Share shall go to the Survivors or Survivor of these. If they should all die as aforesaid, I then give and bequeath the same unto my son William. Item. It is my will that my wife shall have the use of all my household furniture during her natural life and after her decease that the same shall be sold and the Money arising from the Sale thereof be divided between my son and Grandchildren in manner above directed, that is to say, one moiety thereof to my son and the other moiety to my said three Grandchildren share and share alike. And lastly, I do hereby appoint my beloved wife Sarah and my brother-in-law Mr. Edward Duffield to be the executrix and executor of this my last Will. hereby revoking all former wills by me made, declaring this to be my last will and Testament. In witness whereof I have hereunto set my hand and seal dated the Tenth day of October in the Year of Lord one Thousand Seven Hundred and Seventy-five. Ebenezer Kinnersley.

Signed, sealed, published and declared by the above named Ebenezer Kinnersley to be his last will and Testament in the Presence of us who have hereunto subscribed our Names as Witnesses in the presence of the Testator, Peter Dehaven, Elizah Weed, James Watkins.[1]

---

[1] Will Book "R," No. 81 (pp. 123–24), for Philadelphia, Pennsylvania. The Will Book is located at the City Hall; the original will is at the City Hall Annex.

Appendix IV

A Partial Inventory[1]

Inventory of part of the Goods and Chattles belonging to the Estate of Ebenezer Kinnersley late of Philad[a] in the State of Pennsylvania Deceas'd. Taken and appraised in the Manor of Moreland in the County of Philad[a] this first day of September 1778.

Sundry Bonds and State receipts with Interest due thereon to this day Amount to	£1269. 11. 1
A looking glass	4. 10. –
A Library of Books Containing 154 vols.	86. 10. –
An Eight day Clock	30. –. –
A Large looking glass	7. 10. –
A Thermometer	5. –. –
A small Thermometer	2. –. –

Appraised 1 Sept 1778
        John Swift
        John Holmes

[1] This document is with the original will in the City Hall Annex, Philadelphia, Pennsylvania.

Bibliography

I. A CHRONOLOGICAL LIST OF PUBLICATIONS BY EBENEZER
KINNERSLEY (EXCLUDING ADVERTISEMENTS AND NOTICES
IN NEWSPAPERS)

"A Letter from Ebenezer Kinnersley to his Friend in the
Country," *Postscript* to the *Pennsylvania Gazette* for July 15,
1740.
Evans 4536.

*A Second Letter from Ebenezer Kinnersley, to his Friend in the
Country, Shewing the Partiality and unjust Treatment he has
met with from a Certain Committee whose Names &c. are
inserted in the Pennsylvania Gazette, Number 609.* Philadelphia, 1740.
Evans 4537.

*A Letter to the Rev. Mr. Jenkin Jones from Ebenezer Kinnersley,
occasioned by a late Anonymous Paper, published under the
Fiction of a Letter to him from his Friend in the Country; but
is supposed to be writ by some hackney Writer in Philadelphia,
at the instance and by the Instruction of Mr. Jones.* Philadelphia, 1740.
Evans 4538. This publication is not extant.

*A Letter to the Reverend the Ministers of the Baptist Congre-
gations, in Pennsylvania, and the New Jerseys; containing
Some Remarks, on their Answers to Certain Queries, Proposed
to Them, at their Annual Association in Philadelphia, September 14, 1746.* Philadelphia, [1747].
Evans 5981.

123

[*For the Entertainment of the Curious, . . . Boston, September, 1751.*] Broadside: Boston, 1751.

This broadside is perhaps not extant; its existence was recorded in the *Electrical Review* for May 13, 1905, p. 783. At that time it was in the collection of R. Henry W. Dwight.

For the Entertainment of the Curious, . . . Newport, March 16, 1752. Broadside: Newport, 1752.

Copies: JCB, Rosenbach.

For the Entertainment of the Curious, . . . St. John's, April 25. 1753. Broadside: St. John's, 1753.

Copy: LC.

"From Mr. E. Kinnersley, at Boston, to Benjamin Franklin, Esq; at Philadelphia. . . . Feb. 3, 1752." In Benjamin Franklin, *Supplemental Experiments and Observations on Electricity, Part II. . . .* London, 1753.

"Further Experiments in Electricity," *The American Magazine and Monthly Chronicle for the British Colonies,* I (1758), 627–30.

"To the Author of the Account of the College and Academy of Philadelphia, published in the *American Magazine* for October, 1758." *Pennsylvania Gazette* for November 30, 1758.

"New Experiments in Electricity," *Philosophical Transactions of the Royal Society of London,* LIII (1763), 84–97.

A Course of Experiments, in that curious and entertaining Branch of Natural Philosophy, called Electricity; accompanied with Explanatory Lectures: in which Electricity and Lightning, will be proved to be the same thing. [Philadelphia], 1764.

Evans 9708.

"On some Electrical Experiments Made with Charcoal," *Philosophical Transactions of the Royal Society of London,* LXIII (1773), 38–39.

"A Course of Experiments on the Newly Discovered Electrical Fire by Mr. E. Kinnersley of Philadelphia," in I. Bernard Cohen, *Benjamin Franklin's Experiments: A New Edition of Franklin's Experiments and Observations on Electricity.* Cambridge, Massachusetts, 1941.

II. MANUSCRIPTS

First Baptist Church of Philadelphia. "Minute Book, Feb. 4, 1757—July 1, 1769." Deposited at the First Baptist Church, Philadelphia.

Jones, Horatio Gates. "Rev. Ebenezer Kinnersley, M.A., The American Electrician." Historical Society of Pennsylvania.

Keach, Elias, and Watts, John. "A True Account of the Gathering, etc. [Records of the Lower Merion Baptist Church] copied from the original MS by Horatio Gates Jones, begun March 19, 1862." American Baptist Historical Society.

Kinnersley, Ebenezer. Letter to Mrs. Sarah D. Kinnersley, March 13, 1773. Photostat, American Baptist Historical Society.

————. Letter to an unknown person, January 1, 1757. Original, Historical Society of Pennsylvania.

————. Letter to an unknown person, undated. Original, Historical Society of Pennsylvania.

————. Miscellaneous records in the Edgar Fahs Smith Library, the Rare Book Department, and the Archives of the University of Pennsylvania; the Library Company of Philadelphia; the Historical Society of Pennsylvania; and the American Baptist Historical Society.

Kinnersley, William. Student Note Book. Archives, University of Pennsylvania.

————. Letters to Joseph Yeates. Historical Society of Pennsylvania.

Keiter, M. Robert Warf. "Benjamin Franklin as an Educator." Thesis (Ph.D.), University of Maryland, 1957.

Pennsylvania. University. "Minutes of the Trustees." Archives, University of Pennsylvania.

Philadelphia Wills. City Hall, Philadelphia.

Smith, John. "Memorandum Books." Library Company of Philadelphia.

Spencer, Archibald. Documents in the Maryland Hall of Records.

Spencer, David. "Annals of Philadelphia Baptists, 1682–1919." American Baptist Historical Society.

Tuesday Club. "Records of the Tuesday Club." Maryland Historical Society.

Tilley, Winthrop. "The Literature of Natural and Physical Science in the American Colonies to 1765." Thesis (Ph.D.), Brown University, 1933.

Turner, William Lewis. "The College, Academy and Charitable School of Philadelphia; the development of a colonial institution of learning, 1740–1779." Thesis (Ph.D.), University of Pennsylvania, 1952.

Westcott, Thompson. "History of Philadelphia." 32 vols., collected edition from Westcott's serials in the *Philadelphia Sunday Dispatch*, 1867–1884, illustrated with original documents, pictures, and drawings by David McNeeley Stauffer. Historical Society of Pennsylvania.

III. A SELECT LIST OF ARTICLES

Aldridge, Alfred Owen. "Benjamin Franklin and Jonathan Edwards on Lightning and Earthquakes," *Isis*, XLI (1950), 162–64.

Anonymous. "Lectures on Electricity in 1751," *Electrical Review* for May 13, 1905, p. 783.

Broderick, Francis L. "Pulpit, Physics, and Politics: the Curriculum of the College of New Jersey, 1746–1794," *William and Mary Quarterly*, 3d ser., VI (1949), 42–68.

Chapin, Howard M. "Was William Claggett, the clock-maker, an engraver?" Rhode Island Historical Society, *Collections*, XXII (1929), 41–46.

The Clock Club, Albert L. Partridge, Secretary, "William Claggett, of Newport, Rhode Island, clockmaker," *Old Time New England*, XXVII (1937), 110-15.

Cohen, I. Bernard. "Benjamin Franklin and the Mysterious 'Dr. Spence': the Source and Date of Franklin's Interest in Electricity," *Journal of the Franklin Institute*, CCXXXV (1943), 1–25.

———. "The Lectures and Discoveries of Franklin's Collaborator—Ebenezer Kinnersley (1711–1778)," Appendix I (pp. 401–8) in Cohen, I. Bernard, ed., *Benjamin Franklin's Experiments: A New Edition of Franklin's Experiments and Observations on Electricity*. Cambridge, Massachusetts, 1941.

———. "Some Problems in Relation to the Dates of Benjamin Franklin's First Letters on Electricity," *Proceedings of the American Philosophical Society*, C (1956), 537–39.

Cohen, I. Bernard. "The Two Hundredth Anniversary of Benjamin Franklin's Two Lightning Experiments and the Introduction of the Lightning Rod," *Proceedings of the American Philosophical Society*, XCVI (1952), 331–66.

———, and Schofield, Robert. "Did Divis erect the first European Protective Lightning Rod, and was his Invention Independent?" *Isis*, XLIII (1952), 358–64.

Colden, David. "New Experiments in Electricity," *American Magazine and Historical Chronicle for the British Colonies*, I (1758), 165–66.

———. "To Mr. E. K. of Philadelphia," *New American Magazine*, I (1759), 422–25.

Dvoichenko-Markov, Demetrius. "A Rumanian Priest in Colonial America," *American Slavic and East European Review*, XIV (1955), 383–89.

Eddy, George Simpson, ed. "Account Book . . . kept by him [Franklin] during his First Mission to England as Provincial Agent, 1757–1762," *Pennsylvania Magazine of History and Biography*, LV (1931), 97–133.

Espenschied, Lloyd. "The Electrical Flare of the 1740's," *Electrical Engineering*, LXXIV (1955), 392–97.

———. "More on Franklin's Introduction to Electricity," *Isis*, XLVI (1955), 280–81.

Garden, Alexander. "Account of the Gymnotus electricus," *Philosophical Transactions of the Royal Society of London*, LXV (1775), 102–10.

Gleason, J. Philip. "A Scurrilous Colonial Election and Franklin's Reputation," *William and Mary Quarterly,* 3d ser., XVIII (1961), 68–84.

Hall, G. Stanley. "On the History of American College Textbooks and Teaching in Logic, Ethics, Psychology and Allied Subjects," *Proceedings of the American Antiquarian Society,* n.s. IX (1893–1894), 137–74.

Haraszti, Zoltan. "Young John Adams on Franklin's Iron Points," *Isis,* XLI (1950), 11–14.

Heathcote, N. H. de V. "Franklin's Introduction to Electricity," *Isis,* XLVI (1955), 29–35.

Hujer, Karel, "Father Procopius Divis—The European Franklin," *Isis,* XLIII (1952), 351–57.

Jones, Horatio Gates. "Letters of Benjamin Franklin to Professor Kinnersley," *Pennsylvania Magazine of History and Biography,* XIII (1889), 247–48.

Jorgenson, Chester E. "The New Science in the Almanacs of Ames and Franklin," *New England Quarterly,* VIII (1935), 555–61.

Lemay, J. A. Leo. "Franklin and Kinnersley," *Isis,* LII (1961), 575–81.

———. "Franklin's 'Dr. Spence': the Reverend Archibald Spencer (*c.* 1698–1760), M.D.," *Maryland Historical Magazine,* LIX (1964).

MacLaren, Malcolm. "Early Electrical Discoveries by Benjamin Franklin and His Contemporaries," *Journal of the Franklin Institute,* CCXL (1945), 1–14.

Millikan, Robert A. "Benjamin Franklin as a Scientist," *Journal of the Franklin Institute,* CCXXXII (1941), 407–23.

Morse, William Northrop. "Lectures on Electricity in Colonial Times," *New England Quarterly,* VII (1934), 364–74.

Neill, Edward Duffield. "Rev. Jacob Duche," *Pennsylvania Magazine of History and Biography,* II (1878), 58–73.

Porter, Edward G., ed. "Diary of Ezra Stiles," *Proceedings of the Massachusetts Historical Society,* 2d ser., VII (1891–1892), 338–45.

Rittenhouse, David. "Experiments on the *Gymnotus Electricus, or Electric Eel*, made at Philadelphia, about the year 1770, by the late Mr. Rittenhouse, Mr. E. Kinnersley and some other gentlemen," *Philadelphia Medical and Physical Journal*, I, pt. 2 (1805), 96–100, 159–61.

Rogers, Mrs. Henry. "Abstracts of Wills and Administrations of Northumberland County," *Publications of the Geneaological Society of Pennsylvania*, XVIII (1938–1939), 48–61, 193–209; XIV (1942–1944,) 22–33, 150–59, 247–56; XV (1945–1947), 46–69.

Schonland, Basil Ferdinand Jamieson. "The Work of Benjamin Franklin on Thunderstorms and the Development of the Lightning Rod," *Journal of the Franklin Institute*, CCLIII (1952), 375–92.

Smith, Edgar Fahs. "Early Science in Philadelphia," *Pennsylvania Magazine of History and Biography*, LI (1927), 15–26.

Smith, William. "Account of the College and Academy of Philadelphia," *American Magazine and Historical Chronicle for the British Colonies*, I (1758), 630–40.

Waters, Henry F. "Geneaological Gleanings in England," *New England Historical and Genealogical Register*, XLVII (1893), 104–40.

IV. A SELECT LIST OF BOOKS

American Philosophical Society. *Early Proceedings of the American Philosophical Society . . . from 1744 to 1833.* Published as *Proceedings of the American Philosophical Society*, XXII, pt. 3 (1884).

Anonymous. *A Letter to Mr. Ebenezer Kinnersley from his friend in the Country, in Answer to his Two Letters lately published.* Philadelphia, 1740.
Evans 4542.
This publication is not extant.

Barton, William. *Memoirs of David Rittenhouse*. Philadelphia, 1813.

Beccaria, Giovanni Battista. *A Treatise upon Artificial Electricity . . .* London, 1776.

Bell, Whitfield J., Jr. *Early American Science: Needs and Opportunities for Study*. Williamsburg, 1955.

Benedict, David. *A General History of the Baptist Denomination in America*. 2 vols. Boston, 1813.

Benjamin, Park. *The Intellectual Rise in Electricity, a History*. New York, 1895.

Boucher, Jonathan. *A View of the Causes and Consequences of the American Revolution*. London, 1797.

Bowes, Frederick P. *The Culture of Early Charleston*. Chapel Hill, 1942.

Brett-James, Norman G. *Life of Peter Collinson*. London, 1926.

Bridenbaugh, Carl. *Cities in Revolt*. New York, 1955.

————. The Colonial Craftsman. New York, 1950.

————, ed. *Gentleman's Progress: The Itinerarium of Dr. Alexander Hamilton, 1744*. Chapel Hill, 1948.

————, and Bridenbaugh, Jessica. *Rebels and Gentlemen: Philadelphia in the Age of Franklin*. New York, 1942.

Brigham, Clarence S. *History and Bibliography of American Newspapers, 1690–1820*. Worcester, 1947.

Calder, Isabel M., ed. *Letters and Papers of Ezra Stiles*. New Haven, 1933.

Cappon, Lester J., and Duff, Stella F. *Virginia Gazette Index, 1736–1780*. 2 vols. Williamsburg, 1950.

Chamberlain, Joshua Lawrence. *University of Pennsylvania*. 2 vols. Boston, 1901–1902.

Cheyney, Edward Potts. *History of the University of Pennsylvania*, Philadelphia, 1940.

Church, Arthus Herbert. *The Royal Society. Some Account of the "Letters and Papers" of the Period 1741–1806 in the Archives*. Oxford, 1908.

Cloyd, David Excelmons. *Benjamin Franklin and Education* . . . Boston, 1902.

Cohen, Hennig. *The South Carolina Gazette, 1732–1775*. Columbia, 1953.

Cohen, I. Bernard. *Benjamin Franklin: His Contribution to the American Tradition*. Indianapolis and New York, 1953.

———. *Benjamin Franklin's Experiments: A New Edition of Franklin's Experiments and Observations on Electricity, Edited, with a Critical and Historical Introduction, by I. Bernard Cohen*. Cambridge, Massachusetts, 1941.

———. *Some Early Tools of American Science*. Cambridge, Massachusetts, 1950.

———, ed. *Benjamin Franklin: a Letter on Lightning Rods*. Cambridge, Massachusetts, 1942.

Colden, Cadwalader. *The Letters and Papers of Cadwalader Colden* . . . *1711–1775*. 9 vols. (New York Historical Society *Collections*, L–LVI, LXVII–LXVIII, for 1917–1923, 1934–1935) New York, 1918–37.

Crane, R. S., and Kaye, F. B. *A Census of British Newspapers and Periodicals, 1665–1800*. Durham, 1928.

Cummings, Archibald. *Faith Absolutely Necessary, but not Sufficient to Salvation without Good Works*. Philadelphia, [1740].

De Armond, Anna Janney. *Andrew Bradford, Colonial Journalist*. Newark, 1949.

Dexter, Franklin Bowditch, ed. *Extracts from the Itineraries and other Miscellanies of Ezra Stiles, D.D., LL.D., 1755–1794, with a selection from his correspondence* . . . New Haven, 1916.

Dibner, Bern. *Early Electrical Machines*. Norwalk, Connecticut, 1957.

Edwards, Morgan. *Materials towards a History of the American Baptists*. 2 vols. Philadelphia, 1770–1792.

Evans, Charles. *American Bibliography: a Chronological Dictionary of all books, pamphlets and periodical publications printed in the United States of America from the genesis of printing in 1639 down to and including the year 1820* [*1800*] *with bibliographical and biographical notes.* 14 vols. Chicago, 1903–1959. Imprint varies.

Farrand, Max, ed. *Benjamin Franklin's Memoirs, Parallel Text Edition.* Berkeley and Los Angelus, 1949.

Frank, Elizabeth. *Memoirs of the Life and Writings of Lindley Murray.* New York, 1827.

Ford, Paul Leicester. *Franklin Bibliography.* Brooklyn, New York, 1889.

Gaustad, Edwin Scott. *The Great Awakening in New England.* New York, 1957.

Gillette, Abram Dunn. *Minutes of the Philadelphia Baptist Association, from A.D. 1707, to A.D. 1807; being the first One Hundred Years of its Existence.* Philadelphia, 1851.

Graydon, Alexander. *Memoirs of a Life, Chiefly Passed in Pennsylvania* . . . Harrisburgh, 1811.

Hauksbee, Francis. *Physico-Mechanical Experiments on Various Subjects.* London, 1719.

Hays, I. Minis. *Calendar of the Papers of Benjamin Franklin.* 5 vols. Philadelphia, 1908.

Hildeburn, Charles R. *A Century of Printing. The Issues of the Press of the Press of Pennsylvania, 1685–1784.* 2 vols. Philadelphia, 1885.

Hindle, Brooke. *The Pursuit of Science in Revolutionary America, 1735–1789.* Chapel Hill, 1956.

Hornberger, Theodore. *Scientific Thought in the American Colleges, 1638–1800.* Austin, 1945.

Johnson, Allen, and Malone, Dumas, eds. *Dictionary of American Biography.* 28 vols. New York, 1928–1958.

Jones, Horatio Gates. *Historical Sketch of the Lower Dublin (or Pennepek) Baptist Church, Philadelphia, Pa., with notices of the Pastors, &c.* Morrisania, New York, 1869.

Keen, William Williams. *The Bi-centennial Celebration of the*

Founding of the First Baptist Church of the City of Phila-delphia, . . . Philadelphia, 1899.

Labaree, Leonard Woods. *Conservatism in Early American History.* Ithaca, 1959.

Labaree, Leonard Woods, ed. *The Papers of Benjamin Franklin.* New Haven, 1959.

Lewis, Frank G. *Minutes of the Philadelphia Baptist Association, 1763–1811.* Germantown and Philadelphia, 1931.

Lippincott, Horace Mather. *The University of Pennsylvania, Franklin's College.* Philadelphia, 1919.

Lovejoy, Arthur O. *Essays in the History of Ideas.* New York, 1960.

Lyman, Rollo La Verne. *English Grammar in American Schools before 1850.* (United States Bureau of Education, Bulletin Number 12.) Washington, 1921.

MacLean, John. *History of the College of New Jersey,* . . . 2 vols. Philadelphia, 1877.

Maxson, Charles Hartshorn. *The Great Awakening in the Middle Colonies.* Chicago, 1920.

Meisel, Max. *A Bibliography of American Natural History.* 3 vols. Brooklyn, New York, 1924–1929.

Miller, Perry. *The American Puritans.* New York, 1956.

Miller, Samuel. *A Brief Retrospect of the Eighteenth Century.* 2 vols. New York, 1803.

Mode, Peter George. *Source Book and Bibliographical Guide For American Church History.* Menasha, Wisconsin, 1921.

Mott, Frank Luther. *A History of American Magazines.* 4 vols. Cambridge, Massachusetts, 1938–1957.

Mottelay, Paul Fleury. *Bibliographical History of Electricity and Magnetism.* London, 1922.

Pace, Antonio. *Benjamin Franklin and Italy.* Philadelphia, 1958.

Parrington, Vernon Louis. *Main Currents in American Thought.* 3 vols. New York, 1927.

Parton, James. *Life and Times of Benjamin Franklin.* 2 vols. New York, 1864. *Pennsylvania Archives.*

Priestley, Joseph. *History and Present State of Electricity.* London, 1767.

Rice, Howard Crosby, Jr. *The Rittenhouse Orrery.* Princeton, 1954.

Richardson, Lyon Norman. *A History of Early American Magazines, 1741–1789.* New York, 1931.

Roller, Duane Emerson, and Roller, Duane H. D. *The Development of the Concept of the Electric Charge: Electricity from the Greeks to Coulomb.* Cambridge, Massachusetts, 1954.

Sabin, Joseph. *A Dictionary of Books relating to America . . .* 29 vols. New York, 1868–1936.

Schonland, Basil Ferdinand Jamieson. *The Flight of Thunderbolts.* Oxford, 1950.

Shipland, Clifford K. See Sibley, John Langdon.

Sibley, John Langdon (continued by Shipton, Clifford K.). *Biographical Sketches of Graduates of Harvard University . . .* 12 vols. to date. Cambridge, Massachusetts, 1873–1962.

Smallwood, William Martin. *Natural History and the American Mind.* New York, 1941.

Smith, Horace Wemyss. *Life and Letters of Reverend William Smith.* 2 vols. Philadelphia, 1880.

Smyth, Albert Henry. *The Philadelphia Magazines and Their Contributors, 1741–1850.* Philadelphia, 1892.

———, ed. *The Writings of Benjamin Franklin.* 10 vols. New York, 1905–1907.

Sparks, Jared, ed. *The Works of Benjamin Franklin.* 10 vols. Boston, 1836–1840.

Spencer, David. *The Early Baptists of Philadelphia.* Philadelphia, 1877.

Sprague, William Buell. *Annals of the American Pulpit . . .* 9 vols. 1857–1869.

Still, Alfred. *Soul of Amber: The Background of Electrical Science.* New York, 1944.

Stuber, Henry, ed. *Complete Works in Philosophy, Politics and Morals of the Late Benjamin Franklin.* London, 1806.

Sweet, William Warren. *Religion in Colonial America*. New York, 1942.

Thomas, Isaiah. *The History of Printing in America*. 2 vols. Albany, 1874.

Thorpe, Francis N. *Benjamin Franklin and the University of Pennsylvania*. Washington, 1893.

Torbet, Robert George. *A History of the Baptists*. Philadelphia, 1950.

————. *A Social History of the Philadelphia Baptist Association: 1707–1940*. Philadelphia, 1944.

Tracy, Joseph. *The Great Awakening: A History of the Revival of Religion in the Time of Edwards and Whitefield*. Boston, 1842.

Tyerman, Luke. *"The Life of the Rev. George Whitefield*. 2 vols. London, 1876–1877.

Van Doren, Carl Clinton. *Benjamin Franklin*. New York, 1938.

Vedder, Henry Clay. *A History of the Baptists in the Middle States*, Philadelphia, 1898.

Walsh, James J. *Education of the Founding Fathers of the Republic*. New York, 1935.

Weaver, William D., ed. *Catalogue of the Wheeler gift of Books, Pamphlets, and Periodicals in the Library of the American Institute of Electrical Engineers*. 2 vols. New York, 1909.

Webster, Richard. *A History of the Presbyterian Church in America*. Philadelphia, 1857.

Weems, Mason Locke, ed. *The Life of Benjamin Franklin: written by himself* . . . Philadelphia, 1817.

Whitfield, George. *Journals*. London, 1960.

Whitley, William Thomas. *A Baptist Bibliography; being a Register of the Chief Materials for Baptist History, whether in Manuscript or in Print, Preserved in Great Britain, Ireland, and the Colonies*. 2 vols. London, 1916–1922.

Whittaker, Edmund Taylor. *A History of the Theories of Aether and Electricity: The Classified Theories*. London, 1951.

Wilmer, James Jones, ed. *Memoirs of the Late Dr. Benjamin Franklin* . . . London, 1790.

Wolf, Abraham. *A History of Science, Technology, and Philosophy in the Eighteenth Century.* New York, 1939.

Wood, George Bacon. *Early History of the University of Pennsylvania, from its Origin to the Year 1827.* Philadelphia, 1896.

Woody, Thomas. *Educational Views of Benjamin Franklin.* New York and London, 1931.

Wright, Conrad. *The Beginnings of Unitarianism in America.* Boston, 1955.

Index

EK = Ebenezer Kinnersley BF = Benjamin Franklin

137